He is Alive!

The Chad Yale Story

CINDY YALE
with Kris Fehr

He is Alive!

The Chad Yale Story

CINDY YALE
with Kris Fehr

North American Heritage Press

He is Alive!
The Chad Yale Story

Copyright © MCMXCIX
by Cindy Yale

For permissions, or for serialization,
condensation, or for adaptations,
write the Author at the Publisher's address below.

International Standard Book Number: 0-942323-29-7
Library of Congress Catalog Number: 98-066534

Published by
North American Heritage Press
A DIVISION OF
CREATIVE MEDIA, INC.
P.O. Box 1
Minot, North Dakota 58702, USA
701-852-5552

Printed in the United States of America

All profits
from the sale of
"He is Alive!"
will go toward
Support Thru Sports,
a foundation
established to benefit
burn patients.

Thank you

...from Cindy Yale

My co-author, Kris Fehr, for helping me tell this story.

Ramsey Burn Unit for encouraging me to write this story.

All the medical staff who brought healing
to the life of my son, Chad.

Family and friends of Burlington, Des Lacs, Minot, and the
many North Dakota communities as well as those around
the country who sent words of hope, prayed and held benefits.

My family and my husband's family who gave of themselves
so freely to support and encourage all of us during this challenge
in our lives – the love of family is the heartbeat of life.

Pastor Andrea DeGroot Nesdahl, for teaching me
more about faith than I could imagine and setting
an example of how to live that faith.

Candace Beckman and Sue Mitrovich, Odney Advertising;
Candi Helseth, WriteDesign; Al Larson, North American Heritage Press,
for your support and assistance.

Bob Petry, Minot Daily News, and Paris Brenno, Elite Studio,
for the cover photographs.

And most importantly, to Rocky, Scott, and Chad –
I love you each with a passion that cannot be put into words.

...from co-author, Kris Fehr

Allan, Karla, Laura, and David,
for your patience and encouragement;

To Jeri Dobrowski, my friend and colleague, for your
skillful editing and wise suggestions;

To the Bismarck Tribune, for the
initial opportunity to report on this story.

CONTENTS

Preface

Our own business, a home in the country, and the ideal community. We thought we had it made – life was good.

We had worked hard to establish our carpet cleaning business. It took seven years of hard work, lean times, and long days to establish our business in the area. Our goals were to clean carpets like we would want ours cleaned, and to do so in a friendly, professional manner. As our business built with repeat customers, we were pleased that our goals were being accomplished.

We were a team. Both boys worked during the summer, after school, and on weekends with Rocky. I helped with commercial work in the evenings and weekends, but primarily did the bookkeeping and answered customers' calls.

Owning our business gave us the opportunity to create our own schedule and be flexible so we could be there as our boys grew up and attend all their activities. We loved working together, and it worked well for us.

Rocky had grown up living on a farm, and having a home in the country had always been his dream. I had always liked the idea of being in or near a town–not feeling so isolated. Seven acres, adjacent to city limits, satisfied both our needs.

From the front yard, we looked across the valley and a bridge that spanned the DesLacs river. Behind our house across the river was the community park complete with a ball field, camping area, picnic tables, and a rope hanging from a tree branch where you could swing out over the river bank. We loved the peaceful setting, and our boys loved the freedom of being able to make as much noise as they wanted.

Our home was nothing special, but it was ours. With three bedrooms, two baths, and a large living room connected to the kitchen/dining room, it lacked only a family room where the boys could have some space to be with friends. We were in the process of adding on the family room, and planned to add a deck next.

We moved to Burlington in 1980 because we wanted to live close to a big city, but be in a small community. From our conversations with other people, we learned Burlington had a good school system and a lot to offer in the community. Because Burlington only had a population of about 1,200, we knew not only our neighbors but almost everyone else in town. Our boys started kindergarten in Burlington and graduated from the high school.

Our best friends down the street, on the other side of town, or just a few blocks away. We attended the local Lutheran church, and were involved in community events.

The business we wanted, a comfortable home in a rural setting, good friends, a closely knit community, and strong family ties—we thought we had it all, our dream come true.

Then in a split second our lives changed forever.

CHAPTER ONE

Faith On Trial

H OT WATER SCALDED MY HANDS, turning them lobster-red as I scrubbed with antiseptic soap. Glancing at the steam-distorted mirror above the washing station, the face I saw wasn't my own: sunken eyes swollen red from crying, no makeup, disheveled hair.

In my puffy, bloated eyes, I read the fear. It was stark and it was real; I couldn't look any longer.

Quickly, I pulled on the yellow hospital gown the nurses offered me, stretching long, gloved arms into the sleeves. I felt the nurse tie the back together, covering my old orange T-shirt. With a reassuring smile, she led me 25 feet to his hospital room, stopping at the door. Her green eyes turned dark and serious as she pushed open swinging double doors.

For the first time in more than 14 hours, I saw Chad.

My stomach contracted and felt like it dropped to the floor. I felt frozen, yet my feet glided slowly across the tile floor to his bed. My son's motionless figure was swathed in white gauze bandages from head to toe, covering the ugly, life-threatening burns I knew had blistered most of his body.

In the stillness, a ventilator hissed as it breathed for my son, an athletic, basketball-loving 16-year-old. Tubes of red, blue and black connected Chad to machines that beeped with each heartbeat and metered life-sustaining medications.

I couldn't see his face, which was swathed in gauze. Fear – cold and hard as frozen steel – crept with icy fingers around my heart. Tears constricted my throat. Weeping, I clutched the bed railing and cried out to God. I asked Him to heal Chad and give me strength.

Hours before, as we sped toward the Minot hospital from our home, I had promised God to give Him all the glory and honor for our lives. I promised to speak to people about the terrible thing that had happened in our lives and let them know God was there, that He was responsible for saving Chad.

Now standing alone in my son's room, I felt the iciness give way to warmth, as God's ever-present love surrounded me. Huge, invisible arms held me, and I was sure God had spared Chad's life for a greater purpose than a mother's desperate plea. In the early gray of evening, with machines and medicines building a wall between death and life, I believed with all my heart that God was in that room with us.

How quickly life had changed. Earlier that day our family had slept the innocent slumber of trusting children in our home alongside the Des Lacs River and the nearby railroad tracks, eight miles from Minot, in north central North Dakota. It was February, a time when the thermometer typically plunges to below-zero readings and the howling winds bring icy windchills.

For nearly a week, the temperatures had hovered close to 20 below zero. Our home, though, was warm and snug. We'd lived in the country for two years, moving to the rural parcel we loved after owning a home in Burlington for 12 years. Although we'd lived other places, we chose the small community of Burlington to rear our family, build our businesses, and eventually retire.

Rocky and I met at the National College of Business in Rapid City, South Dakota, where we were both going to school and I worked part time in the administrative office. We married January 30, 1971. Rocky served in the Navy, so we lived the first 11 years of our married lives in South Carolina, near the beautiful beaches along the Atlantic Ocean. Our first son, Scott, was born there on October 31, 1974. Chad followed on June 1, 1977. When Rocky finished his military service, we returned to North Dakota.

Rocky, who came from a long line of close-knit farmers, was eager to start his own business: first, home remodeling and repairs, then carpet cleaning. I worked as the bookkeeper. We felt it was important to have flexible schedules so we could spend time together, raise our family, and interact with friends and relatives.

We always were close to our families. But as we grew and had children of our own, we realized the importance of family reunions, holiday times, and living close to aunts, uncles, grandparents, and cousins.

Our church and the Lutheran denomination have always been central in our lives. At Peace Lutheran, which counted about 375 members, Scott and Chad were confirmed and were active in the youth group, Peace Luther League. Rocky served as an usher for many years and lovingly devoted hours to property maintenance. He also served on the church council.

I began working with junior high and high school aged youth in 1987, advising Luther League. Listening to teenagers' problems, riding out the emotional waves, and sharing in their triumphs quickly became my second passion – after my family.

I, too, served on the church council and at one time was elected council president. I was commissioned as a pastoral assistant in 1992. Helping with worship, communion, baptisms, and visiting hospitalized church members fulfilled my desire to serve God in any way I could.

That Sunday morning, February 27, 1994, dawned clear and cold. Living near the tracks we heard trains pass within yards of our home each day, rumbling along as they snaked across northern North Dakota. Oftentimes, the trains' warning whistles and groaning, squealing wheels were the only sounds breaking the countryside's solitude.

It wasn't unusual that at about 6 a.m., with wintry darkness spread over the region, we would hear a train yet barely notice the noise. That morning, however, we joked about it:

"It sounds like that train went through our living room," I said to Rocky, and we both laughed as we snuggled under the well-worn quilt and stack of other blankets piled on our bed.

Moments later, Chad burst into our room. Sandy-haired, lanky and quite independent, he was always on the go. He tolerated high school because it was where he socialized with his friends. An avid sports fan, he was constantly playing, talking about, or watching basketball.

Excitedly, Chad began telling us that the train had derailed and was, literally, in our front yard. Scattered like dominoes, the rail cars were lying all around our home, buildings, and vehicles. For a few moments, we talked about whether anyone might be injured, and what we might do to help.

A lot went through our minds, but the farthest thing from our thoughts was the long journey that would begin when Chad ran outside. We were only thinking of helping others, when soon it would be us who needed help.

With the optimism of youth, Chad joked about how Scott could sleep through anything, including a train wreck! Then, as he dashed out of our room to dress, Chad woke his 18-year-old brother. Scott was living at home while studying to be a teacher. He attended classes at nearby Minot State University, and dreamed of some day coaching high school football.

As I called 911, Rocky and Chad pulled on dark insulated coveralls, heavy work boots and snowmobile gloves. With an icy blast, Chad slammed the back door behind him; Rocky stepped out the front.

Scott dressed quickly in his trademark wardrobe: a pair of well-worn sweat pants. In his haste, he bypassed a shirt. His dark head peered around the corner into the bedroom, then he appeared quietly by my side, still a little sleepy and wondering what we should do. Together, we glanced out the bedroom window; in unison we gasped.

Outside, our world turned an atomic red. As if we were looking through a red camera filter, everything was tinted and yet we saw no flames. A wave of terror came crashing down on me.

"We've got to get out of here," Scott yelled, breaking the bedroom window's inside pane with his fist, cutting his hand. But before we could, the red glow abruptly disappeared. Scott grabbed a winter coat from a hallway rack and we ran outside through the back door, just as Chad had done moments before. Although the temperature was frozen at 20 degrees below zero for the tenth day in a row, I wore only sweat pants, a sweat shirt and boots.

Despite the momentary flash of red, darkness now filled the dawn. Rocky shuffled around the corner of the house, disoriented and incoherent. He said he was okay, but he didn't know where Chad was. No one did.

Then, together we turned and looked toward Scott's pickup. Horrified, we saw Chad, lying in the snow just a few feet away. Wisps of smoke danced lazily above his motionless body.

My body stiffened with horror, my feet seemingly encased in concrete. Chad's dead, I thought. His still, smoldering body told me so. Fear pressed down on us like a vise as we huddled between snow-banks. Wind whipped the tears from our cheeks.

I'd never felt so powerless. I didn't know what to think, I couldn't think, I couldn't speak. Then, in the stillness, we heard a faint, muffled sound. As we watched, I saw Chad's chest move and then I heard it again, a soft moan. He was ALIVE!

Without hesitating, we ran to Chad. He was alive, by the grace of God, he was alive! I knew God was present in our lives and here He was, taking care of Chad when all had seemed lost.

Bits and pieces of his overalls clung, smoldering, on his chest, legs, and arms. Rocky threw his coat over Chad and he and Scott both flung snow on Chad to douse the glowing embers. I stood watching – numb, confused, terrified – and so frightened for Chad.

Somewhere in the back of my mind, I finally realized there must have been a fire or an explosion. Huge snowflakes began dropping from low-hanging clouds and, as if jolting us awake from a nightmare, we recognized the imminent danger of another possible explosion. We turned toward the frozen Des Lacs River, just a few yards from our home, where we could seek protection from any further fiery blasts.

Before we could move, our neighbor, Troy, drove into the yard. Troy, his wife and young children had been renting a small, three-bedroom house from us for about a year. We hadn't known Troy until he moved his family into the house, but they proved to be good people – another example of God's presence in our lives. Even though their's was the closest house to ours, the dangerous explosion and fire mercifully spared them.

Rocky got in the front of the blue Nissan pickup with Troy, and I climbed into the box. As if he'd done it for years, Scott lifted up his brother, cradling him like an infant in his arms, and held him as we sped toward the main road, Highway 2. The wind chilled my face and bit my ears.

Normally, the drive to the highway would have been less than one-fourth of a mile. However, the train was blocking the only crossing, so we were forced to drive two miles through a rural housing area to reach the main road.

With each bump, Chad groaned in pain. The sound cut like a knife through my heart. Chad was moaning, telling Scott he hurt. Scott tried to soothe him, saying "Hold on, Chad. You're going to be okay. *Just hold on.*" Scott continued to tenderly cradle his brother. The short trip seemed to last for hours, although it was a matter of mere minutes. Then we heard the ambulance's wail in the distance, growing louder as it – and help – drew closer. We met on the road and quickly relayed what had happened.

I wanted desperately to go with Chad, to be his support and to somehow protect him. But the paramedics with the Minot Ambulance Service said no. It was best that we give them room to work on Chad, they said, and not distract them. It was agony to give him up, to let him go – alone – to the hospital. Yet as they took Chad from Scott's arms, I felt a sense of relief.

They moved quickly and carefully toward the ambulance. Their faces were a blur and I didn't recognize anybody, yet I knew

Chad was safe in their care. God was present and would ride with them and Chad. Under His guidance, they were working to save Chad's life.

The ambulance screamed away in the early morning stillness, we turned to each other, lost and helpless. I wasn't sure when I'd see Chad again. All I could think to do was pray, but prayer didn't come easy. Our faith had never before been tested like it was at that moment. I knew God was watching over Chad, or he wouldn't have survived the initial blast. I knew He would continue His vigil. We gave Chad up to our Heavenly Father's care.

As the early morning grayness gave way to full daylight, Rocky, Scott and I stood there and held hands. I prayed aloud to God like I never had before. I asked Him to please take care of Chad, and to be with him. Rocky and Scott stood silently, struggling with their own pain and grief, listening as I prayed.

Then another neighbor, Laureen, who was a nurse, took us to the hospital. Silence reigned on that short, eight-mile drive. Laureen didn't say a word; we didn't speak either. Still terrified, I continued my prayers. I promised God again that I'd give Him all the glory and honor for our lives, and that I'd tell our story – and His – to anyone who would listen, and I begged him to please help Chad.

The silence became eerie as we drove to Trinity Medical Center in Minot. As I watched other people driving, I became angry. They knew nothing about Chad's accident and they seemed too happy: driving to work, sipping coffee, applying lipstick at the stop lights. In a matter of seconds, our lives had changed forever. Couldn't they sense our pain? The world went on with its daily activities, with no idea of the trauma we'd suffered. How dare they!

Impatient to arrive at the hospital, I squirmed in my seat. We weren't getting there fast enough. I wanted to jump out of the car and run the rest of the way.

When we arrived at the five-story building in the heart of downtown Minot, I could see that Rocky's head and face had been burned by the same explosion that engulfed Chad. The burns were just beginning to show. He needed immediate medical care and was whisked into an examination room where the staff treated his swelling skin and injected him with medication. Scott, whose right hand was still bleeding from breaking the bedroom window, was ushered into a nearby treatment room. The medical personnel cleaned his cut and gave him a tetanus shot.

Even though I had no cuts or bruises, the nurses insisted they check me over, too. Physically, I felt fine. However, the combined shock and fear of the unknown left me an emotional wreck. While doctors examined the three of us, another team of doctors and nurses frantically worked to stabilize Chad.

After they determined I was okay, I found a telephone and called our pastor, Sam. Someone from the hospital was calling our family and closest friends. Pastor Sam arrived, briefly talking with me before checking with the hospital staff. Then we retreated into a small cubicle just off the emergency room, where the nurses could find us within seconds.

With the door closed, Pastor Sam and I prayed. It was the first time I'd felt safe in several hours. He became my support and I cried and screamed through my anger and frustration. Pacing frantically around the cramped quarters, I kicked one of my snow boots across the room, missing a large, white ceramic lamp by inches and leaving a mark on the wall. My other boot sat on the floor by the worn couch. I briefly considered kicking it, too, but reconsidered because of what had happened with the first boot.

Pastor Sam told me that Life Link III, a specially-equipped air ambulance, would airlift Chad to the Minneapolis-St. Paul Airport, then transport him to St. Paul-Ramsey Medical Center's burn unit in St. Paul, Minnesota. He told me the 16-bed center specialized in caring for and healing critical burn-related injuries.

A nurse came to tell me I could see my husband. Sitting in a white hospital gown on a white paper-covered exam table, Rocky looked as scared as I felt. I noticed his face beginning to swell with angry red burns. Looking at my husband, I could only imagine how much worse Chad must be. Fear and uncertainty returned full force.

A nurse interrupted and asked if I wanted to see Chad. Oh God, yes, I wanted to! But I was so scared! Could I handle it? How bad would Chad look? Would he know me? With questions and fear painted on my tear-stained face, I nodded and she led me to his room.

Eight medical personnel scurried around Chad, who lay with only a sheet covering him. His skin, waxy and black, was a dramatic contrast against the white bedclothes of the gurney. Surgeons had cut away his outer skin layer to accommodate the large amount of intravenous fluids being pumped through his feet and ankles – the only places left where the veins could hold needles. The lights, dials, beeps and hums startled me: more machines in one room than I'd ever seen and all just to keep one person alive. Chad was somewhat conscious, they told me, so he'd know I was there.

My stomach was nauseous, my heart pounded wildly. Even though I was so very scared, I willed myself to be brave for Chad. I swallowed, took a deep breath and I held back my tears.

Ever so carefully, I touched the cool sheet covering his shoulder.

Then I told him he needed to lie still, to let the doctors and nurses do what they must do to help him. Just lie there and cooperate, I said. I told him I loved him, and that everything would be okay. In my heart, I knew it was true. I knew God was right there, holding Chad in His arms, giving him the strength to live. I saw him for just five minutes, then the nurses asked me to leave so they could prepare Chad for the flight to Minneapolis. I never saw Chad again before he was whisked away by the helicopter.

In Minot, the doctors and nurses were anxious to transfer Chad's care over to burn specialists at Ramsey Burn Center. They told me Chad would be loaded onto a helicopter to fly him to the airport, where the high-tech air ambulance was waiting.

Life Link III was a cramped, fixed wing airplane with one seat beside a stretcher-like bed. Inside, the aircraft resembled a mini intensive care unit, with no room for idle bystanders – just the medical team and the patient. Two paramedics, specially trained in critical care, would travel with Chad. Once in the air, they'd continue to fight for his life during the 90-minute flight.

Again, strangers would be responsible for my son and I felt broken that I couldn't be there with Chad. Because of his burns, Rocky was admitted to Trinity in Minot for observation. As a family, we decided Scott would stay with his father so neither of them would be alone after I left. Pastor Sam booked two seats on the next flight to Minneapolis, one for me, one for him. He said we'd be there before Chad arrived, which made me feel a little better.

Members of our families started to arrive. My mom, one of the first, lived just 10 blocks from the hospital, so I asked her to go back home and pack a bag for me. With Mom's soap, shampoo, hair dryer and curling iron, I showered in a small stall in the emergency room. I was cleaner, but because Mom and I wear different sizes – I'm six-feet tall and wear a size 10 shoe, while Mom stands five-feet, five-inches tall and wears a size eight – she couldn't offer me a change of clothes.

I was wearing my favorite – and oldest – blue Yale University sweat shirt with new royal blue pants. My boots should have been trashed years ago, but were so comfortable I couldn't let go of them. And even though it was the middle of the winter, I didn't have a coat.

Relatives and close friends continued to fill the emergency room, offering us support. They told us the entire town of Burlington had been evacuated due to the derailment and a fear of dangerous fumes or more explosions. Terry, a co-leader of the youth group at church, was one of the first people I saw after my shower. We had worked together at church for seven years, and we'd become fast, close friends. I knew him well enough to see my own fears mirrored in his face.

I felt comfortable asking for his coat – his cherished Atlanta Braves jacket that he favored as much as anything he owned. Without hesitation, he peeled it off and gave it to me. My father-in-law, strong and tough as always, dug deep into his pockets to help me with money for the trip. Soon everyone was handing me money: Rocky's brothers, his brother-in-law, my mother, friends. They gave me all they had. Without a purse in tow, I stuffed it in my pockets. I never counted it. I had no idea how much it was. It would, however, be enough for a motel room, food, and airline ticket.

Reports were coming in that our home, our business, vehicles, and the workshops had burned to the ground. We had lost everything we owned.

We'd built garages to house Rocky's woodworking shop and some of our vehicles: our carpet cleaning van, Scott's customized Chevy four-wheel drive pickup, my 1988 Suburban, and Chad's 14-year-old, two-door Cutlass with the leather top. Rocky and I planned to retire on that property. Now they were telling us it was all gone!

The fire had destroyed all our material possessions, but we had each other. We were still a family.

Pastor Sam and I boarded a commercial airplane for the 75-minute flight. The flight seemed endless, and I worried and wept. When we landed in Minneapolis, we hailed a taxi and asked the driver to hurry to the hospital. Speeding toward the hospital, I again felt angry at the people I saw: smiling, laughing, living their everyday lives. I couldn't imagine ever smiling again.

When we first arrived at the St. Paul-Ramsey Medical Center, the hospital's size overwhelmed me. Five stories tall, with construction adding a new wing and a sixth floor, this seemed like a good place to be. Treating about 200 inpatients and 1,500 outpatients each year, the burn unit serves patients from throughout the Upper Midwest including Wisconsin, Iowa, North Dakota and South Dakota. When it opened in 1963, it was one of only 12 accredited burn centers in the United States. Today there are more than 140 such centers, but few are as large and comprehensive as Ramsey.

Even though everything was either white or gleaming stainless steel, the nurses were warm, personable, and friendly. We were soon ushered into a small waiting room, called a family room, in the fifth floor burn center.

The airplane with Chad hadn't arrived yet. It was hard to be positive, not knowing the reason for the delay. The burn center staff tried to reassure me by saying the air ambulance crew was attending to his medical needs, and that I shouldn't be alarmed. But I was impatient and the time dragged.

Pastor Sam thought it was important that we eat supper while we waited for Chad's airplane to arrive. We rode the elevator down three floors to the cafeteria, only to find it closed. We bought a chicken sandwich out of a vending machine and ate quietly. The sandwich was tasteless. I didn't care about eating – I just wanted my son to be okay.

About an hour after we had landed, Chad arrived and was rushed directly to the operating room. Later I learned he had almost died en route from Minot to Minneapolis.

The burn center nurses explained a few things to me, told me Chad's room number, and tried to calm my fears. They said surgery would take two to three hours. Pastor Sam and I waited in the small twelve-by-twelve waiting room that served the entire burn unit. There was a reddish sofa and two overstuffed blue chairs, a television on the wall, and a coffee machine in the corner. Straight-backed chairs lined one wall.

As the minutes ticked by, the walls began closing in around me. I became numb to my surroundings.

Throughout the surgery, nurses walked the short, tiled hallway to report that Chad was holding his own. I felt slightly relieved until a nurse told me Chad's right arm was so badly injured that it needed to be amputated. She explained that the burns to his arm were so severe they were sending deadly toxins into his body that would kill him. Amputating his arm would save his life. I looked at Pastor Sam. Together we stood and, with one of the nurses, walked the long hallway to the elevator which would take us to the surgical area. This was where I met Dr. David Ahrenholz, whose duty it was to explain in full why Chad's arm must be amputated. He was waiting for us, the forms spread on a table and an uncapped pen in his hand. He showed me where to sign.

Putting pen to paper, I scrawled my signature on the surgical release as the tears rolled down my face. I signed my name to the line knowing I was doing what was best for my child. Logically, I knew losing an arm was better than losing a life but emotionally, I struggled with the thought of Chad losing his arm.

Throughout all the waiting and tears, Pastor Sam was at my side. We talked only when I initiated the conversation. I often saw him in silent prayer, his hands folded and his head bowed. Whenever I closed my eyes, I automatically prayed for strength and for Chad's life.

Finally, after a surgery that had stretched to seven hours, I gazed at my son's bandaged body. His six-foot-tall frame rested on a huge bed made especially for burn patients. The bed was filled with silicone beads held up by air. The nurses told me it felt like floating on a cloud and it would be critical to Chad's recovery. His severe injuries reached deep within body tissue where his youthful skin, muscles, and bones had felt the fire's fury. Learning Chad was the sickest patient the burn center staff had treated in years heightened my fears.

Through intravenous tubes, by mouth, and in skin patches, pain medications and powerful antibiotics flowed to dull the excruciating pain and heal his burns. I worried that it might not be enough.

Chad's odds for survival were so slim, the doctors gave him little chance of waking in the morning. While it didn't sound like much, I grabbed onto the only shred of hope in front of me. That small chance and God's power were all we had. I prayed it would be enough.

As I put my hand lightly on Chad's shoulder, I told him he was doing fine and that they were taking real good care of him. I said he would be fine but that he needed to make sure to do everything they asked of him. I knew it would make Chad uncomfortable if he saw me cry and I needed to be positive to aid his recovery, even if it was in this small way. I struggled to hold back the tears.

That first visit after surgery was only for a few minutes, just long enough to reassure me that he was okay. As I prayed for strength to withstand the uncertain future, I felt God's love replace the panic. Yes, this was a good place. Chad would live. As I left, I looked back at his motionless form – machines breathing, medicating, and nourishing him – and I had just one thought: our God is an awesome God!

That first night, I snatched fitful sleep in a chair in the family room. The nurses urged me to go to the hotel just a block away. They promised to call me should anything happen. I couldn't leave my son. I napped. I prayed and I paced, walking a hundred times or more from Chad's room to the family room. In the darkest part of the night, the time just before sunrise, my mind raced with fear, anger, anxiety – wondering about the grim realities. What if God's plan for Chad wasn't the same as mine?

Alone with my thoughts, I felt the need to connect with my family. Several times I called Rocky and Scott, back in Minot at the hospital. Scott's bandaged hand would heal quickly. Rocky had suffered first degree burns on his face and head, he would heal in two to three weeks' time. Sobbing, I told Rocky about Chad's surgery and the amputation. We mourned the loss of Chad's right-handed hook shot, which he painstakingly had practiced, his dribbling, and lay up skills. How could I ever explain that I gave permission to have his right arm amputated?

On the telephone with Rocky, I felt his worry, love, and concern as he affirmed my action. Even though the amputation was necessary to save Chad's life, Scott was struggling with the trauma and couldn't face the reality of his brother's injuries. Somehow, Rocky said, he knew everything would be all right.

Throughout the night and the next several days, we continued to ask "*Why?*" Why did this happen to Chad? He was a good kid. Yes, there were times he didn't always make the right decisions, but he had never done anything to deserve this. Dwelling on the reasons for the accident wouldn't help Chad, so we focused instead on his recovery. God didn't cause the accident, but He could help us deal with the aftermath. We had to move forward.

My anger surfaced many times. It was always directed at the railroad that caused this accident – the lack of safety measures and apparent lack of concern for life. Many times I wanted to lash out at their representatives who maintained a daily vigil with us at the hospital. Sometimes I struggled to be civil, other times I couldn't speak. I often groped for the two crosses I wore around my neck, reminders of God's presence in my life and in Chad's. The wooden cross on a rawhide thong was the trademark of the Peace Lutheran Youth Group. A delicate Black Hills Gold cross, a Christmas gift from Rocky just two months earlier, hung on a short chain close to my throat. This gift I had treasured, and at the same time thought too extravagant, now became an important symbol of our faith and solidarity.

The next afternoon, 36 hours after the fire, Scott and Rocky hopped a commercial airliner and rushed to join me at the burn center. Wishfully, I had lulled myself into thinking, at least on the surface, that Chad's burns weren't as severe as the nurses said. Rocky's appearance shocked me into reality.

Rocky's face was puffy, swollen and turning brown, his eyes peeping out through tiny slits. White bandages wound around his head, in contrast to his dark complexion. Seeing the aftermath of Rocky's burns, I profoundly knew how badly Chad's entire body had been burned. I couldn't imagine anyone looking worse than Rocky, yet subconsciously I knew that under the layers of sterile gauze, Chad's third-degree burns must look so much worse.

Being together again felt good. Rocky, Scott, and I took turns seeing Chad. We were allowed to be with him practically 24 hours a day. We felt Chad could hear us, even though the painkillers kept him heavily sedated. We talked about the weather, gossip and school news, sports updates, what we had for lunch, or what we watched on television. We read each day's influx of cards and letters. And we told him people were praying for him.

Early on, I began to get acquainted with the burn center staff: doctors, nurses, aides, receptionists. Knowing them, I knew this was the best place for Chad. They brought special gifts and a special commitment to saving lives; I felt they really cared about Chad as if he was one of their own children. It made it easier for me to put my child in their capable hands.

The staff chose their profession for personal reasons. Chad's nurse, Ray, a former burn patient and North Dakota native from Carrington, became instrumental in Chad's recovery. In 1972, Ray was rear-ended by a drunken driver traveling nearly 100 miles per hour. Ray had just picked up a friend who was returning from serving in Vietnam. Ray's 1940 Chevy Coupe flipped end over end and blew up. Horribly burned in the explosion, Ray and his friend were both taken to Ramsey, where doctors worked to save their lives. It took Ray eight years to recover because the accident and burns paralyzed his left arm.

The accident was the impetus for his career choice. Ray endured months of excruciating pain because diminishing pain wasn't part of treatment then. He lobbied Ramsey staff to use pain medications, and by the time he finished nursing training, pain control was standard procedure. He had worked at Ramsey 10 years when Chad arrived.

Because of his experience, Ray cared from his heart and from his soul, tender yet tough on Chad when he needed it. He was just the right mix.

Chad's night nurse was Patti: kind, caring, compassionate. Married to Dr. Solem, one of Chad's doctors, Patti often worked in the burn unit. Even on her days off, she called to check on Chad's condition. I couldn't believe that people cared so much!

CHAPTER TWO

Family and Friends

"OUR FATHER WHO ART IN HEAVEN, hallowed be thy name. Thy kingdom come, thy will be done."

Praying in the hospital chapel, a brilliant banner depicting Moses and the Biblical burning bush before me, I paused at the gravity of the words I'd just mouthed. Rocky, seated beside me, clasped my hand and waited quietly.

Their meaning stung me as I paused to consider my faith. I'd been praying that everything would be okay for Chad, yet also saying "God's will be done." Not mine, not Chad's. God's will. Although they are words we speak almost without thinking, at that moment I faced a hard reality. Maybe God's will for Chad wasn't the same as mine.

For a moment I thought back over the past few weeks. Chad and his teammates on the Des Lacs/Burlington Lakers basketball team had been playing their hearts out. Chad was a starter on the junior varsity squad, yet often filled in for varsity games. He was devoted to the team, never missing practice or a game. The boys had fought for, and won, a place in the regional basketball tournament which would begin the next weekend.

But right now, today, Chad was fighting for a bigger prize: his life.

Was it God's will that Chad not play basketball? Was it God's will for Chad to endure this struggle, and for what purpose? Sitting in the chapel, I accepted that I probably wouldn't ever know the answers, and I didn't really need to know. I had given it over to God; Chad was in His hands. That day in the hospital chapel forever changed the way I said the Lord's Prayer.

When we finished the prayer, we reflected on our meeting with Chad's doctors during his second day of hospitalization.

While pleased that Chad had survived the night, the doctors gave us some sobering, horrifying news. Chad had third degree burns over 80 percent of his body; part of his back and the soles of his feet were spared. That meant both layers of skin down to muscle tissue were destroyed, and even some bone had been damaged.

His skin was raw and red with white and black patches. Nerves and blood vessels were burned and would require a long time before the skin could begin to grow and heal from the edges inward. If Chad survived, he'd need countless surgeries to transplant his healthy skin to the damaged areas. Chad's odds of surviving were about one percent. Quite literally, my son had a 99 percent chance of dying.

We chose to focus on the one percent. If Chad was to survive, he needed our positive support to help him make it though his recovery.

The fire had devoured his ears and the tip of his nose, and he'd lost his right arm in surgery. If completely disfiguring my son wasn't enough, the fire's aftermath also caused his eyes to swell shut, and his brain to swell.

"Chad has overwhelming burn injuries. In previous years, he would not have survived," said Dr. David Ahrenholz, the burn center's assistant director. "He would have passed away very quickly. He's lost a limb, muscle and most of his skin. His chances of survival are very slim."

We were shocked to hear it put so plainly. I had convinced myself Chad's burns weren't much worse than Rocky's – it was how I protected myself from the pain I wasn't ready to face just yet. I knew that with God all things were possible, so I held to my faith, and I prayed.

For Chad to survive this ordeal, our faith in God's sovereignty had to be absolutely unshakable so I gave the struggle over to God, freeing myself of the uncertainties so I could concentrate on Chad. Asking that God's will be done also means that we must have the determination to carry out the tasks that need doing. In Chad's case, it meant, no matter how we felt, we would present a positive attitude and allow only positive comments in his room.

During the first week at the hospital, we met Brad, who understood more than anyone the road that lay ahead for Chad and our family. Brad had been a volunteer fire fighter in the small town of Sherwood, North Dakota, and had been burned when he and six others tried to extinguish an oil tank fire nearly two years earlier. Burned over 75 percent of his body, he spent more than a year recovering at the St. Paul hospital where Chad now lay. Brad's brother, Kevin, was burned over 89 percent of his body and died after fighting his injuries for more than year.

Brad was at the hospital for a checkup, his pretty, youthful wife at his side. Wearing a plastic face mask to prevent facial scarring from skin grafts, he told us about his long road to recovery, which gave us an idea of what to expect. More importantly, he offered us hope. He affirmed our decision to stay positive, and told us that while he was in the hospital, no one told him how badly burned he was.

"All I knew was that I was okay and getting better," he said. "No one told me that I could die."

Best buddies, brothers Scott and Chad pose for the camera in 1978.

Brad told us that his family's positive attitude was the key to his survival. We knew that it could work for Chad, too. I thanked God for sending Brad to us at such a critical time. I felt we'd see him again as both he and Chad continued their recovery.

During the first several days at the burn unit, Scott struggled with the reality of the situation. He became despondent whenever he saw Chad's body in bandages and sustained by high-tech machines pumping medications through his system. Just like his brother, Scott was very independent and we knew that forcing him to visit Chad would be disastrous until Scott felt ready to accept the situation and deal with his emotions. We decided to give Scott time to adjust.

Lounging in the burn center's family room, aimlessly paging through sports magazines, vacantly staring at the television screen, all the time Scott thought about Chad. We continually talked about Chad's condition, and I could see Scott's feelings of helplessness giving way to hopefulness as he devised a way he could help Chad heal. The nurses played music to distract the patients from concentrating on their pain, but Scott felt Chad needed some "real" music, something with a beat that he'd recognize. He shopped several stores until he found just the right compact disc player and several country music CDs he and Chad preferred. The nurses obliged, playing Chad's favorites as they went about their daily routines.

Every part of Chad's body above his ankles was covered in white gauze bandages, which had to be changed twice a day. The nurses said this procedure is required for every patient whose burns cover more than 40 percent of the body. It was the most painful part of his daily routine, requiring two hours from start to finish each morning. We weren't allowed in the room during dressing changes. The double doors to his room – #518 – were swung firmly shut and paper covered the windows. During these treatments, I stayed as close as possible to Chad, not leaving the hospital. I usually haunted the cafeteria for breakfast, or made telephone calls from the family room in the burn center.

Even though heavily medicated and semi-conscious, Chad still suffered, especially during the healing bandage changes which exposed his injuries. To avoid infection, nurses donned clean gowns and wore protective masks. Removing bandages, they washed his wounds with warm water, typically around 90 degrees, near the body's normal temperature. To the warmed water they add a chemical similar to household bleach and, although it sounds painful, the nurses said the bleach actually took some of the sting out of the water. The nurses then applied antibiotic ointment to the open sores, then wound layers of fresh, white bandages around his limbs, chest, and abdomen to shut out the infection and seal in the healing.

Skin regulates people's body temperature and, because the fire destroyed most of Chad's skin, the twice-daily baths chilled him until he shook. The nurses worked fast, but it still took two full agonizing hours.

Chad received what Dr. Lynn Solem, the burn unit's director, called "truckloads of narcotics" through his intravenous tubes, by mouth, through his feeding tube and in skin patches to dull the pain caused by exposed nerve endings. One of the medications caused insomnia, which the staff told me actually helps patients forget the pain and trauma and concentrate on healing.

An interview I read in a newspaper quoted Dr. Solem as saying "probably none of them are adequate. Total comfort is an impossibility."

Several days after the accident and on one of his first visits to Chad's room, Scott plugged in the huge black boom box, positioning the speakers for the best sound. Popping in a CD and cranking the volume up high, the way he and Chad liked it, the "Boot Scootin' Boogie" blared as Scott intently watched his brother.

Suddenly, Chad's big toe moved. Amazed, Scott and I looked at each other, then back at the toe. It was tapping in rhythm to the music! Somewhere inside the mummy of white bandages swathed around his thin, charred body, Chad – the music-loving teenager – was alive! It was nothing short of a miracle.

Moving in mysterious and profound, yet simple ways such as this, God affirmed my trust in Him numerous times during Chad's hospitalization. Before the accident, I would never have thought to give thanks for a big toe dancing in syncopation with a common country song. Yet that simple movement proved Chad could hear. There was life inside the bundle of bandages!

Ever since the accident, we had been talking to Chad but we hadn't known for sure if his auditory system had been damaged by the fire. Now, we began telling him everything! We would cite the scores of the Atlanta Braves' games, his all-time favorite team, and Scott diligently read sports stories and scores from the Minot Daily News, our local newspaper. Rocky and I took turns reading aloud the get-well wishes sent by his friends and our neighbors.

Every week Chad was hospitalized, his best friend, Bill, sent a card. Sometimes it was signed simply, "Love, Bill." Other times, there'd be a short message that fit Bill's quiet, reserved personality to a "t." Although the boys had opposite personalities, they had been almost inseparable since they became friends during third grade.

Every time we opened one of those special cards from Bill, a memory fell out. Before moving from Burlington to our home out-side of Burlington, Bill, who was an only child, and his parents lived just three blocks from our house. During their grade school years, baseball cards were the rage. Bill and Chad always seemed to find enough extra money to buy one more pack of cards, and they spent hours debating their worth, trading and getting together with other boys and their boxes of cards, haggling for hours to make the perfect trade.

Bill and Chad loved All Star Wrestling, especially Hulk Hogan. They'd watch it, or baseball, on television for hours and argue about whose team was better: Bill's Minnesota Twins or Chad's Atlanta Braves.

In school, Bill studied and pulled good grades. Chad, loud and outgoing, only allowed grades to take priority over socialization during basketball season when he needed passing grades to keep his spot on the team! The night before the accident Bill and Chad had been together. Chad's accident shattered Bill's life, too, and he

Chad and his best friend, Bill, celebrate Bill's birthday in 1988.

would be seen gazing at Chad's locker before and after basketball practices. The circle of friends had been broken when Chad was sidelined.

Bill was critical to Chad's healing. We'd read that special card to Chad day after day until the next one arrived. Bill or his parents, Phil and Karen, called each Thursday night to find out about Chad's progress and to bring us news from home. We looked forward to those calls so we could tell Chad about it the next day. We'd always tell him, "Bill says hi."

Sometimes we'd ask Chad if he remembered us telling him about the calls, the cards, or sports scores earlier in the day. He might respond with a slight nod of his head, which encouraged me. But there were also times when there was no response.

Chad has Attention Deficit Disorder, which I often ruefully referred to as selective hearing for teenagers. Many times, Chad seemed deaf to my admonitions to wear his jacket, take extra money, to be home on time – only to remember the things that were the most important for him to recall.

I thought back to a few days before the accident. Chad yelled as he passed the kitchen that he and three pals were going for pizza after basketball practice. I ran after them, reminding Chad to be home early because his school books were stacked, unopened, on his desk and he needed to study. He nodded absently. I knew my message fell on deaf ears and he didn't open any of those books.

How trivial that all seemed as I sat at his bedside, prompting Chad to remember things he'd never have forgotten before the accident – the day of the week, sports scores, news from home. He didn't always remember the days of the week or what we'd told him earlier in the day so I was encouraged when he'd remember something!

During the second and third days, our families and close friends had arrived to become an active support system. The telephone in the family room rang constantly with people from home asking about Chad. My sister, Kathy, started a journal for me that listed callers' names and notes about their calls. So many people called that the hospital's telephone lines jammed, mostly with calls from the Burlington and Minot area. It reassured us even more to know so many people were concerned about Chad.

Telephone calls also came into the hospital from all over the country. That's when we realized the national news media was printing and broadcasting our story. At first we weren't happy about the coverage. We were very private, uncomplicated people. For us, it was a personal issue, but to the media, it was news.

Like a proverbial double-edged sword, we also knew that the more people heard about what had happened, the more they would pray for Chad. We had become a front-page newspaper item, a media event. And while we didn't have to like it, we worked to turn it around in Chad's favor.

The media wanted to meet us, to hear our story. But even before we granted our first interview, in the midst of our shock and grief, the cards and gifts began arriving from people living all over the United States and Canada. Nearly every one wrote that they were praying for us, praying for Chad. We heard about prayer chains in southern churches, on the West Coast, and back home.

Thousands of people prayed for Chad's recovery. It was a humbling experience to realize people we didn't know, along with friends and relatives, were lifting our child up in prayer. Many times each day I thought about the old saying, "It is easier to give than it is to receive." We were used to giving; but accepting support was much more difficult.

Gifts and cards from Chad's friends and classmates began arriving days after he entered Ramsey. One of his friends sent a pair of red, size ten basketball shoes I had put on layaway until I could pay for them all at once. Others sent an Atlanta Braves jersey, and his own #42 warm-up jersey from school.

Preparing for the day when his swollen eyelids could open, we hung the shoes by their laces to the bar on his bed, where they dangled in Chad's line of sight. We hung the jerseys, caps, and cards on the wall across from his bed and on the ceiling so he could see them, too. When he opened his eyes, he would know people were thinking of him and praying for him.

Sometimes I'd gaze at the shoes and think how, hanging by a shoestring, they paralleled Chad's life held together by prayer. At these times, when it was incredibly hard to keep a positive outlook, I'd just let the tears silently wash down

Scott and Chad anticipate Christmas in 1981.

my face. Speaking would have betrayed my emotions so I kept my silence. Chad couldn't stand to have me cry over anything.

On March 2, five days after the accident, the nurses excitedly reported a milestone to us. Chad helped lift his own head off the pillow as they unwrapped it during the usual bandage change. Other than the toe-tapping, it was the first indication we'd had that Chad was aware of his surroundings and daily routine. We gave thanks for his determination. He would need it; he was scheduled to begin a series of surgeries the next week.

CHAPTER THREE

Special People

WHILE SO MANY PRAYERS FOCUSED ON CHAD, God saw that our whole family needed help and support, too. Often, when days seemed darkest and Chad's healing was an abstract concept, He sent his earthly messengers to our family. Through such special people, we came to know God's hand in our lives.

Within days of the accident, Scott decided he needed to be with us – and with his brother – more than he needed college. He dropped out of Minot State University and put his life on hold so he could be at the hospital full time. We lived in a hotel room two blocks from the hospital so we could be at Chad's side in minutes no matter what time of the night. On an average day, we spent from 8 a.m. until 11 p.m. at the hospital.

Even though our story was very public, we wanted desperately to keep our privacy so we could maintain some semblance of family life, too. Pat, the hospital public relations director, helped us greatly by screening calls so only certain people would be able to reach us in the hospital's family room. The hospital switchboard and the burn unit staff didn't release our hotel name or telephone number, either. Oftentimes, if we weren't at the hospital and visitors showed up, the unit would call us and we'd walk to the hospital. To keep our privacy, just our families and very close friends knew exactly where we were staying.

The hotel staff protected our privacy, too. They wouldn't put through calls to our room without checking with us first. From the housekeeping staff to the manager, everyone seemed genuinely concerned about our family. Having quiet time alone gave Rocky, Scott and I time to deal with this upheaval in our lives, and the chance to make critical decisions regarding Chad's future.

Back home in the Des Lacs-Burlington High School, the 46-member junior class started a decorating campaign. They'd weathered the first few emotional days, with school even cancelled one day so the juniors and seniors could talk about their emotions after the accident, evacuation and Chad's condition without the distractions of school work. Now, though, the kids needed to do something.

From end-to-end, the students publicized their faithfulness to Chad. Red posters bearing his name and basketball jersey number, along with slogans like "No Fear Chad Yale" and "We Miss You, Chad" filled nearly every available space in the school. The elementary school held popcorn parties to raise money, while at the high school, the kids video taped the school day for Chad, decorated lockers, made and sent cards and planned fund-raising events. Hungry for information, the school at first announced news about Chad. Later, the secretary compiled regular information sheets. When the news was positive, the kids cheered and high-fived. When we'd had a setback, they fell silent.

The high school principal, Alton Nygaard, had his hands full discouraging kids from driving to the St. Paul-Ramsey Medical Center. They didn't understand how close to death Chad still was, and they wouldn't be allowed to see him even if they managed to obtain permission to make the trip.

"They needed to become aware of what they'd see – the appearance of what a fire does to a body," Mr. Nygaard said.

So he arranged for the volunteer fire fighters from Sherwood, North Dakota, to speak to the students. The Sherwood Five, as they came to be known, had answered a call to an oil tank fire west of town, and were trying to circle the blaze when the wind shifted. Seven team members were caught in the blaze and two of the men later died from their injuries. They were all horribly burned and spent months in the very hospital where Chad now lay.

The men spent a day at Chad's high school, talking to students about recovering from burns and answering their questions. They spoke openly, Mr. Nygaard said. Their message: If you don't know, ask questions. It helped Chad's friends to learn what he'd look like when they saw him again, and how his life would most likely change, just as the fire fighters' had.

We were grateful for the school's assistance. We didn't yet know what the long-term reality of Chad's burns would be, but the kids back home were demanding answers. While I called the school about twice a week with updates, I had my hands full keeping up with Chad's medical needs, answering the telephone and trying to re-establish a household.

Rocky's cousin, Cathy, and I slogged through a local discount store, each of us pushing or pulling a huge cart heaped with a montage of necessities for daily living: shampoo, hair dryers, socks, underwear, shirts, makeup, razors...we cruised up and down each aisle.

Normally, I enjoy shopping. But trudging back to the stores, day after day while Chad fought for his life, was a chore. People stared at us and at our piled-high shopping carts. Part of me wanted to tell clerks and other customers that the fire had consumed every material thing, all the possessions our family had owned. But the rest of me wanted solitude.

Cathy was literally a godsend to us. Growing up, she and Rocky had lived about six miles apart. A strong and independent soul, so much like myself, Cathy was a person I'd liked instantly from the moment we met 25 years earlier and we had continued to see her at family events over the years. She lived in the Twin Cities of Minneapolis and St. Paul, and visited us often while we were at the burn unit.

Cathy was one of the special people God sent when our lives were in disarray. She seemed to show up at just the right times, bringing a fresh breeze to our sometimes stale and stagnant routine. She kept us supplied with food, games, books, stationery and even stamps for responding to those who were writing to us. Cathy's greatest gift, however, was her stamina and common sense that she applied so many times when we were re-equipping our family.

Jacki and Terry, who had given me his jacket at the Minot hospital following the accident, had become our best friends more than a dozen years earlier. We met through the church where Terry and I eventually became the Luther League advisors. Our families were always close, with lots of late night pinochle games, traveling to school activities and summer backyard barbecuing together. Jacki and I would talk on the telephone for hours. We called it "imparting information to each other" while our husbands dismissed it as "gossiping."

During those first horrible days following the accident, they were almost as worried as we were and called as many as six times a day. Finally, Terry just showed up at the burn center. He stayed with us for two weeks, taking time off from his job, while Jacki stayed home to care for their young sons. People back home knew our families were close friends, so Jacki and Terry's telephone rang almost non-stop with hundreds of telephone calls during the first week of Chad's hospitalization. One day, Jacki told me her new motto was "Help, I'm on the phone and I can't shut up!"

Jacki and Terry were among those back home whom we trusted to distribute accurate information for us.

Another was Paula, a true friend whose sons are the same ages as Scott and Chad. At one time, Paula had coached Chad's elementary school t-ball team so she knew him and his pals. In fact, she once said he was a "strong, stubborn, headstrong young man." Well-known in our community, Paula spoke candidly. I knew I could count on her to dispel rumors, not spread them, and to give folks the right information. Paula called us at least twice a month and lifted Chad up in her daily prayers. She also helped organize the Yale Support Group to remind our community about Chad and his continuing need for prayer.

I'll always cherish Penny, the mother of two of Chad's and Scott's classmates. She surprised me by popping into the burn unit one day on her way through town. A nurse at the district health unit in Minot, Penny and her husband, Mark, own and operate their own business where they employ their two daughters – much like we employed our sons in our carpet cleaning business. Penny understood a little of Chad's medical situation and knew we needed encouragement.

On her brief visit, Penny gave me a light brown, cuddly teddy bear about 18 inches tall. Her thoughtfulness helped; I carried him wherever I went. I hugged him a lot, his soft fur and cushy stuffing a tangible reminder that with God all things are bearable, all things are possible.

Donna was studying to be a pastor at Luther Theological Seminary in Minneapolis. I met Betty and her through the pastoral assistant program when we spent a week at the seminary. Both of them felt called to the ministry through that program, and they had teased me that I should think about the seminary too. I told them I'd stay with youth ministry and leave the preaching to them.

Betty, who was studying at Wartburg Seminary in Dubuque, Iowa, came to visit. And Donna gave me a dark blue Bible that became very important to me as I often read from it while sitting next to Chad's bedside. More than anything, I read to distract myself and pass the long days in the hospital.

As our friends and close relatives flooded into the burn unit, news of Chad's condition began to trickle out. The media was hungry for any tidbits about Chad: his condition, what he'd endured so far, and what lay ahead for our family. Misinformation began circulating around Burlington and I realized that it was now time to put a human face on Chad's suffering, on the devastation of our property, and on the forced evacuation of everyone from our small town.

Pat, a tall, broad-shouldered man whose soft, kindly voice seemed the exact opposite of his imposing height, was the hospital's media relations director. During the first few days, he screened media calls and answered reporters' requests.

The hospital's first official press release about Chad's condition came on March 1. For our first interview, Pat contacted the CBS television affiliate in Minneapolis because the story would be broadcast at home, and the St. Paul Pioneer Press. Quite honestly, he told them we weren't emotionally able to talk about some things and they agreed not to press us for information if we appeared uncomfortable. To their credit, the reporters never asked insensitive questions. The hour-long interview went very well, although Rocky and I were nervous and ill at ease telling strangers about our tragedy.

After that first interview, we conducted many more, both in person and over the telephone, for national and hometown media. The motivation for telling our story wasn't to gain fame; we already had national recognition by virtue of the circumstances surrounding the train derailment. But people were concerned. It was time to stop the rumors about Chad's condition and to let people know that he wasn't out of the woods yet. We also wanted everyone to know that we needed their continued prayers and support for Chad.

Every time we did an interview I asked people for their prayers. And, almost like clockwork, we were deluged by mail from across the country after the story was printed or broadcast. About 40 cards and letters arrived each week, some with inspiring messages, most bearing signatures of people we'd never met or knew. We learned that Chad and our family were being remembered in hundreds of prayer chains across the United States.

As strange as it sounds, it felt a bit uncomfortable to learn the scope and magnitude of the prayer groups. We didn't like holding center stage, being known only for the great tragedy that happened in our family. But we also knew that for Chad to recover, he needed prayer and lots of it. So, each time we did an interview and whenever the hospital released information about Chad's condition, we asked people to remember Chad in their prayers.

It was immensely difficult to remain upbeat every day. Often, Rocky and I retreated to the medical center's chapel, on the main floor of the hospital. A small, narrow room, with a dozen or so pews in a row down the middle, and aisles on either side, it was a cozy, reassuring refuge.

Rocky and I often went to the chapel to pray and wait for the results of Chad's most recent surgery. At the close of each day, I'd stop to thank God for all that had happened and to ask for strength for the coming challenges. Here, away from the eyes of everyone else but God, I could turn my burdens over to Him.

I sought out the chapel's refuge – and its safety – to release pent-up frustrations. Oftentimes, my need to be alone came at odd hours. At first this caused a problem because the chapel was unlocked only during certain hours. Several times during Chad's first weeks in the burn unit, I had to call a maintenance or security staff person to open the doors.

One day, Chaplain John handed me a key to the chapel.

"You know, Cindy, I think you just need to have a key so you can come and go as you need to," he told me. "When you're done with that key, you just return it to me."

After an especially difficult day at one point, Chaplain John included Chad in the closing prayers. Then, he pushed the button on the tape deck and played "We're Family," one of the songs that was popular with the youth back home at Peace Lutheran.

We're family.

I need you and you need me. We're family.

Brothers and sisters standing side by side…

Memories flooded back to me as I remembered singing that song with both my sons during a more carefree time that seemed so far removed from the now-daily presence of pain. I couldn't keep the tears from streaming down my face.

As I continued to cry, I sensed the presence of someone at my side. Hesitantly, I turned, and saw Pastor Andrea DeGroot singing with me, her tears matching mine. Pastor Andrea was the assistant to the bishop in North Dakota; she had been a great friend and influence in my faith journey and in my youth ministry work. She was someone I'd striven to emulate, whose strong faith fed mine, who agreed with my heartfelt belief that working with youth was an important service.

More than 1,000 cards and letters, crossing all denominational and theological lines, found their way to us. Cradled in God's arms, we felt protected as details of our suffering became the topic for conversations between folks we'd never meet. We were, and continue to be, grateful for the prayers that we know saved Chad for some greater purpose in this world.

CHAPTER FOUR

With a Little Help from Your Friends

AMID CHEERING FANS and a band jauntily hammering out the teams' school songs in the District 15 basketball tournament, a heavy silence hung in the Des Lacs-Burlington locker room. Separated by distance, but close-knit in spirit, the Lakers stood in silent meditation for their absent comrade. It was March 7, eight days after the accident.

Chad, a junior varsity squad starter, had averaged 10 points per game throughout the season. He sometimes bolstered the varsity's ranks and had practiced long and hard for tonight's tournament where they'd play the nearby Surrey Mustangs. Instead, he lay in a drug-induced, semi-conscious state hundreds of miles away.

The gravity of Chad's condition wasn't lost on his teammates; they had debated forfeiting rather than playing the district tournament. Their coaches let them make the decision. The strapping youngsters finally decided to play, knowing it was what Chad would have wanted. They dedicated the game to Chad.

"It's kind of emotional," Coach Doug Wagner told a reporter covering the tournament. "Some are visibly upset. Some hide it better than others. I told the kids win or lose, that's secondary."

When they ran onto the hardwood floor, they all wore a small number 42 – Chad's number – on their uniform straps. One of Chad's closest friends, also named Chad, wore his friend's jersey instead of his usual number 14. Fans shrieked their approval as the Lakers warmed up.

"We're best friends," Chad's friend told the same reporter. "He'll always be with us. I felt proud and honored to wear his number.

Known as a strict non-conformist, Chad never did things quite like anyone else, especially if his coach or another adult told him how to do it. He didn't particularly care what others thought about his appearance, and often wore one black sock

Chad playing basketball in fifth grade.

pulled up almost to his knee and the other pushed down to his ankle. When they played at the district tournament, several of his teammates did the same, a testament of their link to Chad.

Chad's friends played their hearts out for their friend and they won the game, 46-43, taking fifth place in the tournament.

The tournament was the first of many community fund raising events for our family. We heard that tournament officials talked to the crowd about Chad's condition, and then placed three pails for donations at different corners of the basketball court. Officials later reported that fans had donated more than $2,500 which went directly to a bank account set up for our family.

I also heard about one of Chad's young cousins, Katie, a precocious seven-year-old, who had been saving her allowance and birthday money to buy a special horse figurine for her collection. She and her parents walked into the local Wal-Mart store, where they noticed a 10-gallon fish tank out front with coins and floating dollar bills. Intrigued, they stopped to look at the tank.

Katie asked the obvious: "Why is money floating in the water?"

Her parents, Rocky's brother and his wife, explained that the store was collecting donations for Chad, to help him get well. Katie hesitated only a moment, then dug deep into her jeans pocket and plunked all her money into the aquarium.

She didn't buy the long-saved-for horse, but her generosity in giving all she had moved me to tears. In ensuing months, as Chad remained hospitalized, we heard about other fundraisers to help our family. It was then that we came to understand the saying, "It is easier to give than to receive."

Chad and his fifth grade basketball team in 1987.

The Yales' love of sports has always been evident, like in this family photo, taken in 1989.

About the same time, the Peace Luther League began making buttons in support of Chad. In colors of the rainbow, they read either "Praying for Chad" or "Friend of Chad" along with his junior class picture in the middle. Knowing that Chad's friends from the youth group were backing us and uplifting us in their prayers bolstered our optimism.

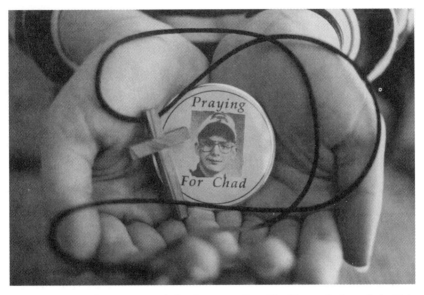

The small wooden crosses and the "Praying For Chad" pins bolstered the Yale family's optimism.

Back in the burn center, Chad's days were filled with a different kind of conditioning, his daily burn care. One of his favorite nurses, Becky, was a 12-year veteran of the burn unit. Patient, caring, and kind, Becky had a brother Chad's age so she took a special interest in Chad.

Becky guided Chad through his days filled with x-rays, CAT scans, temperature taking, blood tests, and, of course, the painful, daily cleansing and rebandaging of his burn wounds.

Within a week of Chad's arrival at the unit, the staff inserted a feeding tube into his small intestine to assure he was receiving enough nutrients. Every day posed a new battle against infection and other complications. The doctors told us Chad's brain was "somewhat" swollen due to all the trauma his body had endured. It was normal and nothing that really concerned them. However, it surely worried me to know that his brain wasn't its normal size.

On March 8, nine days after arriving at Ramsey, Chad was back in the operating room. His eyes had been swollen shut from the trauma, but that morning, one opened. It was just a tiny slit, but Chad could see us. Wow!

My heart soared. Chad could actually see us, not just hear our voices.

During the surgery, doctors cleaned off more burned skin. Then they placed skin donated from cadavers, called an allograft, on the burned areas of Chad's body. The cadaver skin, while a temporary covering, shielded his body from dehydration and infection, while his fragile nerve endings healed. The burn center staff called all over the county to locate enough cadaver skin to cover Chad's burns; and they even considered using pig skin, a very common covering for severely-burned skin.

We often take our outer layer of skin for granted, although it's a first-class sensory organ essential to our survival. I gained a new appreciation for skin during the time Chad spent in the hospital. Skin regulates internal temperature, restricts bacteria entry into our bodies, helps remove waste, prevents dehydration, and protects internal organs and muscles. An adult has about 18 square feet of skin weighing about six pounds and averaging about .04 to .08 inches thick.

Also during surgery, they removed a small piece of healthy skin about the size of a quarter from Chad's back. This was sent to an

East Coast laboratory where it was grown into two-inch pieces they'd eventually graft onto Chad's body. Called cultured skin, it costs $660 for a piece the size of an ordinary soda cracker and takes about three weeks to yield enough skin to cover two to three square feet of burned skin. Cultured skin is extremely fragile, sunburns easily, is never as durable as the original skin, and doesn't sweat. It turned out to be a different color than Chad's healthy skin. Chad would require repetitive procedures to add this new skin, and he would have to care for it in a special way for the rest of his life.

During his second week of hospitalization, Chad's kidneys started to fail and weren't cleaning his blood. In almost total failure, with his blood pressure bouncing from low to high, Chad was in grave danger. We called dozens of people and asked for their prayers to help Chad through his kidney problems. Little by little, hour by hour, his kidneys slowly rebounded. Things were looking up.

Chad remained in critical condition with stable vital signs. His temperature stayed elevated for many weeks, but doctors told us it wasn't too unusual considering the severity and amount of surface area burned.

"It's a slow recovery, but it's what we expected," Dr. Solem told us.

He said Chad's progress was small, comparing it to going up a long mountain. We compared it to a narrow tunnel we'd just entered: too tight to turn around, not far enough in yet to see anything but the faintest hint of light. But it gave us hope, even though Chad remained in critical condition. He'd stay that way, Dr. Solem said, until 65 percent of the burned area was covered with his own skin. We had a long way to go.

The burn center staff worried about Chad's inactivity, which can lead to shrinking skin and a loss in range of motion. On March 10, 12 days after his arrival, therapists began stretching and moving

Chad's burned skin. The exercises would comprise his rehabilitation for months to come. The physical therapists' first goal was to try to move all five fingers on his remaining left hand. Much to their amazement and our relief, all five fingers flexed.

Chad's eyelids, which had been reconstructed from skin on his scalp, needed stretching, too. Chad was persistent in moving his eyelids, because if he didn't work them, they'd shrink. As he slowly closed his eyes and opened them as wide as possible, I thanked God that Chad was able to understand what he needed to do. Soon, he was able to do even more. By March 18, less than three weeks after his arrival, he was rolling his body slowly from one side to the other to help with his baths and the bandaging, and he lifted his head off the pillow more and more often. He could also communicate with the nurses if he needed more pain medication by nodding his head in response to their questions.

It was about this same time that the nurses began weaning Chad from the ventilator which had breathed for him since he'd entered the burn unit. The machine made it impossible for him to speak, but he needed to build up his strength gradually before they could disconnect it completely. He struggled a little at first to breathe on his own. Breathing uses a lot of energy, so at night Chad used the ventilator so he could rest, saving his energy for the next day's therapy and treatments.

CHAPTER FIVE

God's Blessings

WELL-WISHES from Sunday School classes and grade school children splashed red and green and blue against the stark, white walls of Chad's hospital room in the St. Paul-Ramsey Medical Center's burn unit. Posters of the Atlanta Braves and dozens of cards plastered the room. Everywhere possible, we placed visible reminders of the support flooding in from across the North American continent. Cards and letters continued to pour into the hospital mail room.

Chad's eyes were still swollen partially shut. Soon the surgeon would sew them closed to help stretch the new skin while his face continued to heal. Because he wouldn't be able to see anything after the surgery, we hung brightly colored messages everywhere within his line of sight – cards, posters signed by Sunday School students from California to Maine, and by everyone at Des Lacs-Burlington High School, ball caps, and other gifts. His red shoes still hung on the bed, and we even used the ceiling space overhead for display space. Chad needed to know, in more than words, that a legion of friends and relatives – even people we didn't know – were praying for his recovery.

Besides inspiring us all, we wanted the well-wishes to soften the harsh, sterile whiteness of the bandages, bedding, walls, and bathroom fixtures in Chad's room. Not that we faulted the hospital in the least, but the drab color scheme sometimes became overwhelming, threatening upbeat feelings we might have.

During these down times, I retreated to my Bible for God's messages of healing. "I am with you always" became a recurring theme. To know it was true, I needed only to look at the "Thinking of All of You" banner in red, foot-high letters to know that God, through thousands of friends and strangers, was truly with us.

The Minot area's monthly blood drive was nearing and my friend, Paula helped organize a blood drive dedicated to Chad. He had received numerous transfusions during and after surgeries, so it wasn't uncommon for us to see a red pint bag hanging from the IV pole next to his bed.

"People want to help Chad, and there isn't much they can do," the blood services director told a newspaper reporter. "But this is something they *can* do and it could help the next person who needs blood in the hospitals."

Forty-seven people donated blood the first day of the drive, and many more donated in Chad's name in the following days. They called it a "living memorial to Chad," and we supported that idea. By God's grace, Chad had survived to this point. We wanted to be able to let others know that and, at the same time, we wanted to help others. All the blood donated during the drive remained in the community.

Before the accident, Chad had adopted the new No Fear slogan, writing it on the back of some of the T-shirts he wore for basketball practice. It quickly became a favorite with Chad and his friends, as it did with many teenagers across the country.

As his English teacher once said, Chad always wanted to accomplish the goal, whatever it was, by himself. Independently-minded, he liked to figure things out on his own, and rarely asked for, or accepted help.

One day, a T-shirt that spoke to Chad's determination arrived from his classmates:

absolutely

positively

most definitely

without a doubt

NO FEAR

(not even a little bit)

We hoped the T-shirt's message – that he could fully recover and that everyone believed it possible – would inspire Chad. So, with high hopes we hung it, along with his red basketball shoes and Atlanta Braves ball cap, straight across from the head of his bed. And we looked for the smallest of signs that Chad was recovering. It wasn't a long wait.

Before the accident, Chad lived on pizza and Diet Coke. For Chad, Diet Coke was the "real thing," his beverage of choice. But he'd had little but ice chips to taste for almost a month. On March 21, I asked his nurse, Ray, if Chad could sip some Diet Coke.

"Yeah. We need to bend the rules a little bit," Ray said, smiling. Having been a burn patient, he understood that small things can make big changes happen. It seemed that he knew instinctively this gesture might jump start Chad's lagging spirit.

Ray popped open a cold can of pop, poured a small amount into a white plastic cup, and drew it into a syringe. Then, as I watched intently, he wedged the pop-filled syringe between the bandages and dribbled the Diet Coke onto Chad's tongue. He drizzled several small tastes, careful not to spill even the slightest drop.

Although Chad's face was swathed in white gauze except for his eyes and a small opening for his mouth, I knew he was smiling. The slits in his eyelids crinkled slightly, and for a brief moment, I glimpsed a shadow of Chad's heart-warming grin. From that day until Chad left the hospital, he and Ray shared a special bond. By meeting one of Chad's non-medical creature comforts, Ray began building a trust that would be central to Chad's recovery.

A week later, on March 27, we celebrated four weeks of Chad's new life. A day hadn't gone by that I didn't thank God for my son and for his progress in overcoming this monumental challenge. I also thanked Him for the nurses and doctors because I saw God healing Chad through them. They had become a staff manned by angels and miracle workers.

Even though thoughts of Chad filled most of my waking hours, I was still aware of the great suffering around me. Every day I asked God to be with the other burn patients and their families who, like us, agonized with a friend, spouse or relative. Being at the burn center all day every day, I came to know the families of many patients and, because we shared common bonds and burdens, I came to know some of their stories.

I'll always remember Bennie, a diesel mechanic who lived just 25 miles from us. He had been burned over 75 percent of his body when a diesel tank he was welding ruptured. We hadn't known Bennie and his wife, Shannon, before Chad's accident, yet we became acquainted at the burn center. Bennie was only 22 years old; Shannon was pregnant with their second child. A devoted wife, she stayed by his bedside, watching television, working crossword puzzles, and tending to Bennie. They were an inspiration.

One day Bennie decided he was going to walk, despite being warned by the medical staff that such activity would be too painful. He did it anyway, walking around the circular nurses' station. I admired the young family's determination, yet I knew from talking with Shannon that Bennie's path to recovery wasn't an easy one. I watched the physical changes and emotional struggles she endured with a badly-burned husband, a one-year-old, and a baby due five months after his accident.

Hope was another memorable patient, burned in a Minneapolis car accident and saved from death when a stranger pulled her from the car. Her mother visited daily, and we shared and prayed together.

Todd, a rancher from southwestern South Dakota, came to the burn center when a propane heater exploded while he was warming a baby calf.

Perhaps most heartbreaking of all was the baby burned by scalding water. The nurses carried her around to soothe and comfort her because she was too young to talk.

When speaking with people in the family waiting room, the conversation invariably turned to religion. I shared my personal perspective that our God is an awesome God, and that His presence was being felt in Chad's life, and in my own. I truly believed God was at work in the burn center, and that He was lovingly watching over each patient and his or her family.

Time seemed to move slowly, though, and for many months Chad would remain the sickest, the most severely burned, of all the patients.

On March 31, a month and four days after our nightmare began, Chad entered the operating room for his sixth operation. The surgeons would be cleaning off more burned skin and sewing Chad's eyes shut to protect them during the healing process. We told Chad he wouldn't be able to see after surgery, but that it was only for a short time, and the procedure was necessary for him to get better. We encouraged him to visualize his colorful surroundings until he could once again gaze at the outward signs of love and concern surrounding him.

Before he was wheeled down the hallway and into the elevator for the descent to the operating room, I bent close to Chad's head. I searched his eyes, already closing drowsily from the effects of the pre-surgery anesthesia. I fixed the sight in memory and murmured a prayer for his safety. Wiping away the tears, I left the room as Rocky shared his own personal message with Chad.

In the corridor, Rocky and I clasped hands and walked toward the elevator. With his free hand, Rocky used his thumb to press the down arrow on the call button. When the doors opened we stepped into the elevator and made our way to the chapel. We would wait there in silent prayer and meditation until Chad returned from surgery.

CHAPTER SIX

Support from Home

"HI MOM."

On April 4th, for the first time in two months, I heard the voice, barely above a whisper, that I'd longed to hear. I'd prayed and waited to hear those words again, just as I'd anticipated his first words as a baby 16 years ago. It was one of the first signs that Chad's recovery would take a slow, steady path rather than progressing by leaps and bounds.

Before the accident, Chad was very talkative around his friends and, like most teens, reserved his deepest feelings and thoughts for those friends. An independent thinker, he'd defend his friends when we questioned him, and he insisted on winning family arguments. If Chad felt he was right and we were wrong, we were never able to resolve the dispute.

Since Chad usually had the last word, his prolonged silence caused an enormous void in our lives. His whisper was a great milestone, although beginning to speak again while connected to the tracheotomy was a tricky affair. To be able to speak, Chad was disconnected from the ventilator, which meant he also had to breathe on his own. Since speaking required extra effort and Chad was still in critical condition, he wasn't allowed to speak more than a word or two at first so he could conserve his energy. Over time, the therapist increased the time to two or three hours, three times a day.

The speech therapist helped Chad to speak and pronounce his words with a tracheotomy – a hole in his throat where the staff attached his ventilator – since it is so different from the way most people talk. The adaptive device, called a speaking valve, screwed onto the end of his tracheotomy and assisted him with speaking. Made of white plastic, it was about three-fourths of an inch long and about the diameter of a nickel. The first day Chad actually spoke, I was out of the room when he counted to five out loud for Rocky. He was thrilled and so proud.

Chad's first conversations with his father and me were short ones, usually about the weather, his cards, upcoming treatment and other daily topics. When he and Scott were together, they talked about friends back home – gossip, school news, and sports. He avoided talking about the accident and we didn't initiate that conversation.

By now, Chad was awake most of the day, nodding yes or no to the music choices presented by his nurses. He smiled at their jokes, but it was Ray who frequently brought a quick grin to Chad's face. He teased Chad when the Atlanta Braves played poorly or lost a game, and he'd produce another smile when he talked specifically about a game or particular play.

But not every day was as joyful as when Chad first spoke. At times, he slept two or three days in a row, showing no reactions to anything. Many times, although I kept reading him the cards from home and retelling parts of Atlanta Braves games, Chad didn't respond or acknowledge my presence. There wasn't a smile, or a nod, or a response to anything we told him. My hopes dashed, I sat quietly crying, staring blankly at the wall. Perhaps he was depressed, or maybe it was his teenage mood swings which stood in the way of his recovery.

I conferred with Chad's doctor about his moodiness and excessive sleeping. He pointed out that most ill people do sleep an extraordinary amount, and that I shouldn't be overly concerned. That reassured me. With both Chad and me having up and down days, the roller coaster ride of emotions was difficult for Rocky and Scott.

Following the advice of Brad, the Sherwood fire fighter we met soon after we arrived at the hospital, we hadn't told Chad how severely he was injured. By early April, about six weeks after the accident, we decided that Chad needed to be told about the extent of his injuries. We asked Becky, who had a wonderful rapport with Chad, if she could tell him. The experience was too fresh and traumatic for me to relive. I knew I couldn't handle telling my son that he'd never again dribble a basketball or shoot his perfected right hook shot, not to mention he'd need to learn to write with his left hand.

For several days in a row, Becky asked Chad if he wanted to know about his medical condition. He always shook his head, indicating a "no." She said he probably had guessed, because she'd seen him reaching with his left hand to touch his right arm and he often wiggled his right shoulder as if it itched or he was shrugging off a pesky insect. Chad wasn't yet ready to accept his loss or the severity of his accident, Becky said, but I shouldn't worry about it because people handle losses differently.

"He just wants to know where he's at and that he's okay. He doesn't want to see the full picture yet," Becky said. "But that's all right. He's a strong person."

Despite the reassurances from doctors and nurses, I worried about Chad's attitude once he recovered. While I knew that our lives were changed forever and that Rocky and I would spend years caring for Chad, I wondered how Chad would react to and deal with his limitations.

"It's all based on how Chad accepts what's happened and how he chooses to deal with it," Rocky told me as we discussed whether to force Chad into some sort of counseling. We agreed that our son needed to accept his injuries so he could help himself recover.

One morning, Becky again asked Chad if he wanted to know what had happened to him. Although he didn't respond, she told him all about it, including the loss of his right arm just above the elbow. Becky told me each time she explained more, they both cried. They cried off and on throughout the day as she explained the devastating effect the fire had on his body, and about his present limitations.

Chad now seemed ready to accept his injuries, and he more fully understood what he needed to do to recover. We started to see his attitude begin to improve. One weekend, Chad's cousin Shawn was visiting from South Dakota. Although three years younger than Chad, the two had always been buddies, especially when he'd spend time with our family during the summer. When Shawn visited that weekend, he asked Ray if Chad could move his feet. Chad didn't have his speaking valve, but before Ray could answer, Chad vigorously wiggled his toes. It was his way of letting his cousin know he could hear him. And that he didn't need Ray to answer for him.

We eventually decided that Chad's independence would hinder any therapeutic efforts unless he made the first move. The psychologist we consulted told us to remember that Chad now had few choices because so much of his existence had been snuffed by the accident. He told us to give Chad as many choices as possible, allowing him to make simple, everyday decisions that helped him assume some control over his life. Did he want the television on or off, did he want his cards read to him, would he like some ice chips or a Popsicle?

Scott was the most patient family member in giving Chad choices and allowing him time to answer. With just the two brothers alone together, their relationship blossomed and took on a new dimension. Scott read Chad's lips or asked questions, and patiently waited for Chad to nod yes or no, sometimes calmly repeating the choices if Chad didn't respond. It seemed Scott intuitively knew what Chad needed, yet he waited for Chad to tell him.

On April 8, four days after Chad spoke his first words, the doctors wheeled him into the operating room for surgery number eight. This time, they would place cultured skin – Chad's own skin, that quarter-sized piece taken from his back in an earlier surgery and grown in a laboratory – over parts of his body where earlier operations had removed burned skin. Extremely fragile, cultured skin is shipped on an airplane where it rides in first class and is rushed to the hospital for immediate implanting. Since it isn't very durable, the doctors told me they wouldn't place it on knees, elbows or other joints because normal wear and tear would make it necessary to replace it. Those parts of Chad's body would have to be covered by his own skin, in the form of a skin graft from his back or his feet.

During this first cultured skin procedure, the surgeons placed 57 squares, worth more than $37,600, on his body. Chad was out of the operating room by noon, which was a little sooner than anticipated. Since things seemed under control for the moment, Rocky decided to return to Burlington for the first time since the accident. Scott remained with me in St. Paul, but I still felt uncomfortable that Rocky and I would be separated.

Four days later, Chad was back in the operating room. The cultured skin so carefully grown and placed on his body had dissolved or been rejected by his body. The doctors told me this wasn't uncommon; in fact, Dr. Ahrenholz told me he expected only about 40 percent of the tissue to stick. He said successful grafting would be crucial to Chad's recovery, and would require patience. During this surgery on April 12, doctors covered Chad's body with 162 more cultured skin squares, valued at about $107,000. It was more successful this time, with 70 percent of the skin actually adhering to his body.

During Chad's first ten weeks in the hospital, his bills tallied a staggering $845,262 for all the surgeries, medicines and extremely specialized care. Although we had medical insurance, we only saw one bill – and that was by mistake. Our insurance company was never billed. The railroad paid all medical bills, instructing the hospital and hotel to bill it directly. It was a burden lifted so we could concentrate all efforts on healing Chad.

In addition to his surgeries and learning to speak again, Chad began physical therapy twice a day during the week and once on Saturday. The exercises were designed to stretch his arm, legs and back joints and muscles, along with lifting his head. Stretching the new skin was important because burned or grafted skin tends to shrink and tighten.

After receiving an extra dose of pain medication, Chad would lie flat on his back in his bed for the session, which lasted 30 minutes to an hour. At first, the therapist slowly lifted Chad's left arm off the bed and gradually flexed the elbow, wrist and finger joints until each could bend and stretch normally.

The extremely painful regimen tormented me. I couldn't bear to watch Chad wince and pull away in pain as the therapist persisted. In my heart I wished the therapists would leave him alone, but I knew that Chad needed the therapy to improve. Even if it was painful for him, I could see Chad making daily progress.

I often wondered how the therapists could continue their jobs which put patients through such agonizing pain, day after day. The therapists said they know the stretching process, however painful, is the only way for the patient to recover. They knew their efforts were for the patient's own good.

While I visited with others in the family room or paged through a magazine to divert my mind from the therapy, Scott would stay by Chad's bedside. Along with the therapists, they encouraged Chad by reminding him that if he wanted to use his arm, legs, shoulders, hips and feet, he needed to cooperate. He understood and while he didn't like it, he complied whenever he could.

Our lives continued the wild roller coaster ride, with Chad progressing well for several days, followed by a day when things fell apart and he slipped backward. Sometimes his vital signs weren't as good as they should be or his temperature was slightly elevated, which signaled an impending infection. Surgery days were nearly always positive because Chad was strong enough to tolerate the operation – and it also meant one less operation in his future.

Following skin grafting, Chad had to lie still for four or five days so the grafts had time to stick. But the lack of activity caused his healing skin to shrink and draw taut. His progress would back-slide and physical therapy would start again from square one. Riding that emotional roller coaster nauseated me. Some days I couldn't hold down food, and it was difficult to even force a smile. Sometimes, I became angry when others would laugh or joke. Even seeing another burn patient leave for home would annoy me. Although I was glad to see them recover, Chad still lay in bed fighting for his life every single day. It didn't seem fair.

It was a frustrating and uncertain time. I prayed. Physically, I was alone. Chad's pain and moodiness and Scott's quiet demeanor weren't compatible with my downhearted spirits. Rocky was still back home, tending to our business. Although we kept in touch daily by telephone, it wasn't the same as having him by my side.

CHAPTER SEVEN

Daily Struggles

CLOUDS OF STEAM ROSE FROM THE SINK and blurred the mirror as hot water gushed from a faucet outside of Chad's room. I watched my hands again turn lobster-red, washing away the bacteria and viruses that could endanger Chad's life if I carried them into his room. We'd gone through this procedure when Chad first arrived and now, the middle of May, we were doing it again. Chad had a staph infection.

Rocky had been gone just six days; I was thankful he returned so quickly when Chad's condition worsened. Together again, I felt we were stronger. We readily accepted the familiar routine.

Before going into his room, we needed to wash with special antiseptic soap and wear hair nets, rubber gloves, blue face masks and yellow gowns. We kept ourselves covered like this all the time we were in Chad's room and when we came out, we threw the outfits in the garbage. Suiting up one day, I remarked to Rocky that we looked a little like twin Big Birds with blue beaks. We laughed, momentarily breaking the tension. One-line jokes were a way we tried to keep a sense of humor in the face of continual setbacks.

Another day, I coaxed a smile from Chad when I told him yellow wasn't my best color. "It isn't the only color of clothes I've got;

I have things I wear under this. When I can quit wearing this gown, you're going to see all kinds of new outfits," I said, smiling behind my mask. Chad rolled his eyes, a common, unspoken gesture that let me know his sense of humor was intact.

Trying to find humor in such a desperate situation wasn't easy. Earlier in the month, we had thanked God for the successful plastic surgery on Chad's eyes. The swelling had decreased, the pads came off and both his eyes opened. Chad had been listening to the television for weeks and now he could actually see the baseball games and talk shows, and all the cards decorating his walls. He could see everything and his attitude improved.

Our happiness was short-lived, however. Soon after the eyelids operation in the first week of May, Chad went back to the operating room for skin grafting. It was his 12th trip and this time, the doctors removed a layer of skin from his feet and ankles to graft to his legs and buttocks. Because so much of Chad's body was burned, he had very little good skin to peel off for grafting. It was a mistake to use skin from his feet. Even before the accident they were ultra-sensitive to touch, so the procedure left him in agony. The nurses gave him extra doses of pain medication during the bandage changes, but it made little difference. For about three days, the intolerable pain distracted Chad so that it seemed nothing else went right.

Chad needed to lie motionless for up to five days for the grafts to take. In the meantime, progress made in physical therapy suffered. It was a constant battle that wore down our resolve, and we were mere spectators. For Chad's sake, we knew we had to win this round.

One weekend in May, my sister's family from South Dakota was visiting us at the hospital. When my 11-year-old niece, Renae, came to the family room after seeing Chad, her little face looked pale and her chin trembled. I asked what had happened.

"I felt like crying but the tears are in my stomach and they won't come out of my eyes," she said.

I gave her a big hug. That's how I felt most of the time, I told her. It's okay to feel sad, I said, but remember that God is going to heal Chad. He'll recover. Even as I spoke the reassuring words, I felt their truth surge through my heart. I held on to that feeling, tears stinging my closed eyes, during the coming days when Chad's pain and suffering continued to trouble me.

Now that Chad was more alert, he began asking for us as soon as he awoke each morning. Sometimes that was before 8 a.m., which amused us because Chad had always loved to sleep late into the morning. Even if it was for just a few minutes, he wanted to see someone from his family before his morning routine of burn care and bandage changes. We'd hurry to the hospital to wish him a good morning, then grab a cup of coffee in the family room or head to the basement cafeteria for a pancake or caramel roll breakfast.

He insisted that either Scott, Rocky or I be in his room all the time, to distract him from the pain as much as to keep him company. His cramped room already held an over-sized hospital bed and an assortment of monitoring equipment. With all those machines, and the three of us wearing our protective clothing, the room felt extremely warm. We decided to take turns visiting. Using a rotation system gave Chad a change of company and gave the rest of us a much-needed break, a chance for a walk, and some fresh air.

Physical therapy resumed despite Chad's additional pain caused by skin grafts taken from his feet. We were eager to help, and the therapist showed us how to assist Chad with his eye exercises and how to stretch his fingers. Whenever one of us was in the room, we'd instruct Chad to hold his eyes shut, open them as wide as he could, then close them again. He'd complete five or 10 repetitions, as prescribed by the therapist, then we'd read his cards or talk.

To work his fingers, Chad needed to make a fist and hold it to a count of five. Then, he'd slowly extend his fingers, stretching them toward the Atlanta Braves poster on the wall. He'd go through this exercise up to 10 times, rest his hand, then repeat the process several times each day. With both his eyelid exercises and his hand stretching, we could see improvement. Chad noticed it too. The nurses said they often saw Chad working on either his hand or his eyelids on his own, without anyone reminding him to do it. His determination to get better inspired me and eased some of my worries about his attitude.

Thinking back to our first days at the burn unit, I remembered talking about Chad to the mother of another burn patient, Hope. We shared a bond because of what our loved ones were experiencing as they recovered. We also found comfort in the constant stream of telephone calls and visitors who kept up our spirits.

Chad smiles for his sixth grade school picture.

Hope's mother and I had reminisced about our children, and I'd told her about Chad's determined, stubborn personality. "One of those tough kids," she had commented, as I thought about how Chad's attitude used to frustrate me.

She reminded me that God gave him that disposition, and that He did it for a reason. I wondered how a more mild-mannered patient might have fared under the same circumstances. Sitting in the cramped family room, curled in my favorite reddish easy chair, a smile crept across my face as my mind drifted back.

I had often struggled with Chad's stubborn ways. When he was younger, we assigned chores that needed to be finished before he could play with his friends. They were simple things like cleaning his room, straightening the closet where his clothes and boyhood treasures intermingled in heaps on the floor, washing dishes, vacuuming and mowing the grass. Chad always waited until the last minute to get started, then became frustrated when he wasn't finished and his friends were waiting.

"Just let me go this one time and I'll finish as soon as I get home," he'd plead.

"Sure, Chad, we've been through this a million times," I'd say skeptically. Often, though, my softer side prevailed and I'd relent. Later, we'd argue about his still undone chores.

At times Chad served detention in school for talking out of turn, or when the teacher had declared a blanket silence for the class. He had all kinds of excuses. It wasn't his fault; someone asked him a question first; he merely answered and the other person didn't get in trouble.

It seemed he waited until the last moment for everything. He'd start a report the night before it was due and he'd be running down the street at 7:45 a.m., missing the bus that left at 7:40 a.m. Then Rocky or I would grudgingly drive him the eight miles to school. On the way he'd remind me he had a basketball game that night and "Oh, Mom, my uniform is in my gym bag and it's dirty."

Many times Chad's actions made me terribly angry and I even told him, "I love you all the time, but I don't necessarily like you." Chad just laughed. Seldom serious, Chad was always in the middle of things, talking, living on the edge. Somehow, he knew, everything would turn out okay despite his last-minute efforts.

In the hospital after the accident, I thanked God for that frustrating, strong-willed disposition, and reminded myself that God doesn't make mistakes. He gives us all the skills we need to survive.

CHAPTER EIGHT

Baby Steps

WARM WATER RUSHED OVER CHAD'S LEGS and up his torso, immersing him in his first real bath in 10 weeks. A true milestone, this first out-of-bed bath was a longed for event. The bath would be a regular experience unless he'd had recent skin grafting, then it was mandatory confinement to allow the grafts to heal.

Getting Chad into the bath was awkward because he couldn't yet walk. So, on May 16, the nurses lifted him off his special bed into a hammock-like sling that they rolled down the short hallway to the tub room. I could see that being lifted out of bed and scrunched in the sling caused great discomfort. However, Chad was anxious for his bath and wasn't going to let pain stand in his way.

Once in the bath room, the nurses used the sling to lower Chad into the soothing warm water. The successful experience relaxed Chad for the remainder of the day, during which he complied with his therapy and seemed to be less irritable with us and the hospital staff.

Just three days before his successful bath experience, the physical therapist introduced Chad to a mouth spreader. Using this spongy device, which looked like a small, flexible, hollow tube filled with a dense pink sponge, was difficult at first because the new skin around Chad's mouth had tightened. Without the spreader, he couldn't fit a teaspoon into his mouth and it barely opened when he spoke.

In the beginning, Chad used the soft tube for just a few minutes at a time. It was uncomfortable, and he couldn't speak, so he would read or watch television. It took days of diligent stretching before Chad's mouth could open wide enough for a teaspoon. In time, the therapist hoped to work Chad up to wearing an adjustable metal spreader with rubber pads on each end. He would need to wear it all time except when he was eating.

The Saturday following his first bath, Chad lifted his right leg about an inch as the nurses were preparing him for another experience – being out of bed and sitting in a recliner. Since Chad had been lying on his back for two and one-half months, he had to gradually get used to sitting up. That first day, he spent just two hours in the chair, which was fully reclined. The next day it was a little longer and the angle adjusted upward, all depending on how Chad felt. It was good to see him direct some of the recovery steps, which helped him gain more control over his life.

As Chad was progressing toward sitting up all day, his best friend, Bill, came to visit. Bill and his parents drove 10 hours straight to St. Paul on a Saturday, arriving at the hospital just after lunch time. The boys spent a few hours together, talking about sports and friends, before the family needed to leave for the long journey back to Burlington. Chad's face lit up when we read Bill's cards, which he mailed weekly, or when we mentioned that Bill or his family had telephoned. Seeing his best friend in person did wonders for his recovery.

Sitting up helped increase Chad's endurance. He soon could lift both of his legs about 12 inches off the bed. And, on May 25, about three months after the accident, he took his first sip of water from a cup.

For the past several weeks, Scott had been returning to Minot during the week to start piecing his life back together. He found an apartment and a job working in a friend's construction firm. He hoped to return to college in the fall. Every Friday afternoon, Scott boarded a commercial flight for St. Paul, where he devoted his weekends to his brother. Sunday night, he'd return to Minot where his girlfriend, friends, job and apartment waited.

Chad lived for those moments when Scott strode through the door with a big smile and all the news from home. Chad became animated, chuckling softly as he heard about his friends' latest antics and as he related what he could remember of his hospital activities during the past week. On Sunday nights, within an hour or two of Scott's departure, Chad gradually shut down. He became quiet and pensive, already missing a vital link to the life he hoped to someday reclaim.

One Sunday in May, I was crocheting in the family room while Scott and Chad visited. Scott poked his head around the corner and said, "Mom, you're supposed to go in and see Chad now."

I walked into the room. My usual greeting vanished as I stared in disbelief at Chad's chest. A delicate Black Hills Gold mother's ring lay there sparkling in the light. I gasped and tears ran down my face. I had almost forgotten it was Mother's Day. I wanted to hug Chad, but it would have been too painful for him. With tears trickling down his face too, he motioned for me to try it on. It was a perfect fit!

"It's beautiful! Thank you! I love it," I said. Those simple words said it all, yet somehow seemed inadequate.

I walked to the family room, where Scott sat quietly, a slow smile playing on his face. The tears again ran down my face. Rocky, other patients' families and the nurses crowded around and demanded to know what was happening. For the last few years I had hinted that someday I'd like a mother's ring, but the idea hadn't even entered my head since Chad's accident and hospitalization. If anyone had asked me, I'd have told them I already had everything I wanted – my family was together. Later, Scott told me Chad and he had cooked up the surprise during his weekend visits, not even telling their father.

That same month, Chad told me he wanted to graduate with his high school class the following year. I couldn't believe that the kid who studied only enough to make the basketball team wanted to talk about his academic future. He was already several months behind his junior class and we weren't even talking about when he might leave the hospital for good. I wasn't sure he could catch up, considering his previous disinterest in school and his physical limitations. My hesitation was short-lived as I remembered his tenacity. If he set the goal, he'd probably accomplish it.

With the hospital's help we located Cliff, a tutor on staff at the children's hospital connected to the St. Paul-Ramsey hospital. Normally, Cliff worked only with much younger students but he made an exception for Chad. Working with a high school student and different material would be a new challenge for him, but he was willing.

Teachers at Des Lacs-Burlington High School sent textbooks and assignments in social studies, literature and English to Cliff each week. Cliff read Chad's lessons to him, asked him questions about it, gave him an oral test, then sent the test results back to Chad's teachers. Cliff was a wonderful teacher, patient and kind, able to work with Chad's attention deficit and the physical problems that prevented him from reading or writing. Chad looked forward to his tutoring sessions even though they consumed his day along with physical and speech therapy sessions and regular medical care.

With Scott coming and going, and friends visiting, Chad soon became eager to walk again. Before that could happen, his feet had to be desensitized to feeling the pressure of shoes again. Under the therapists' direction, we began placing slippers or socks on his feet, over the Ace bandages that encased them. The nurses told me to buy Chad shoes a size or two larger than his normal 10½ so they would fit over the bandages. It wouldn't be long, they said, before his feet would shrink back to their usual size and he could wear the red tennis shoes hanging from the bed.

Since he'd only wear them for a short time, I told Scott I'd probably just buy an inexpensive pair of size 12 or 13 shoes from a discount store. Scott had other ideas.

"No way," he said. "Chad's not wearing anything that's ugly. He's not wearing a crappy, cheap pair of shoes!"

After thinking about it, I decided Scott was right. If a "cool" pair of shoes could help Chad walk sooner, then it was worth spending the extra money. I found a pair of basic white Nike shoes in a Minneapolis sporting goods store. Scott put his stamp of approval on them and Chad liked them, too. The next hurdle was putting the shoes on his ultra-sensitive feet.

The first day we put one shoe on, and it stayed on for less than five minutes. Chad gasped with pain and the monitors in his room skyrocketed to their maximum levels. The next day, the nurses again placed his foot inside the shoe. This time, he tolerated the pain a few minutes longer. That afternoon, it stayed on even longer. On the third day, both feet wore shoes. Soon, he was up to wearing them for 30 minutes at a stretch. We told Chad that wearing shoes would help him accomplish one of his goals: to walk again. In just a week, he was wearing both shoes several hours a day.

On the down side, Chad was still in bed, still on his back. Until now, the hospital staff had lifted Chad out of bed and placed him in the chair. Now he needed to be in an upright position to put pressure on his feet. On May 26, the male aides and a therapist rolled a slant board into Chad's room, lifted him onto the hard surface and secured straps around his torso, legs and arms. Then, the therapist turned the crank to elevate Chad's head so some of his body's weight was on his feet.

The day's goal was to see what degree of tilt Chad could tolerate. We expected it wouldn't be much after lying in bed for almost three months, maybe 10 degrees at the most. Marked by fear and apprehension, Chad's face lost some of its color, and he grimaced. Rocky and I composed ourselves, holding back our emotions. Watching our son go through so much pain, day after day, took its toll, but we knew it was necessary. As the table raised Chad's head, we grimaced along with him. After a few minutes, he would reach a 10-degree angle to the floor.

The therapists increased the angle slightly each day. Although Chad moaned and cried with each additional degree of tilt, he wouldn't quit. Within weeks, Chad could tolerate a 45-degree angle to the floor and lie in that position for about five minutes. Chad defied his doctors by accomplishing more than they thought possible in a short period of time.

Later, when I went to the hospital's chapel, I thanked God for working his many miracles in Chad. I knew that he would recover, and I felt that God saved Chad for some greater purpose than simply enduring the grueling road he traveled. Reflecting there in the chapel, the thought suddenly came to me that God was working through Chad and might do so for the remainder of his life. It was a humbling thought, yet one that comforted me. God had already taken over Chad's struggle and He wouldn't let his trials be in vain. The inspiration helped me accept yet another surgery; Chad was scheduled for his 14th trip to the operating room the following day.

This time, we were apprehensive because they would graft skin from Chad's back to his face and begin the cosmetic changes that would take months to complete. His back had fairly good skin that wasn't badly burned. Even though the skin was his own and available for collecting, it would be a tough surgery. When it was over, Chad's appearance would have changed from what we had grown accustomed to. And, he'd have a metal halo screwed into his head to keep him still and in one position.

Following the operation, the doctors told us everything went according to plan. They peeled three flaps of skin from his back and attached one to the middle of his face, one on the left side of his face and one on the right side, overlapping them at his chin. Hundreds of black surgical staples secured the transplanted flesh. Fervently we gave thanks to God for his guidance and for allowing the surgery to happen so flawlessly. Clasping hands, Rocky and I eagerly walked to the elevator. Rocky punched the button to take us to the fifth floor, where Chad lay heavily sedated from the surgery.

Even though the doctors had told us the extent of the procedures, we were ill-prepared for what we saw when we walked into Chad's room. It was a ghastly sight. My baby's face was red and bloody, and he had a huge, mechanical-looking metal halo on his head that was fastened to the opposite corners of his bed. The grafted skin was reddish-brown, with tiny staples holding it in place. Thankfully, he was sound asleep and would remain heavily medicated for several days to lessen the discomfort from facial skin grafting.

Evidently I gasped because the three nurses in the room all turned to look at me at once. They were smiling proudly.

"It's beautiful, Cindy. It's just a masterpiece," one of them said. "Dr. Ahrenholz does the best work. It's perfect!"

From their comments, I knew it must be good. They had seen similar skin grafts many times before, and knew what they were talking about. All I could do was stare in disbelief and trust that God knew what He was doing.

C H A P T E R   N I N E

Happy Birthday

"HAPPY BIRTHDAY TO YOU, happy birthday to you! Happy birthday, dear Chad. Happy birthday to you!"

Chad was hardly aware of his birthday. He was still fighting for his life, fighting to see what his life was going to be. Birthday cards flooded into the hospital as folks back home remembered. But Chad was too sick, still too sedated, for us to read many of them to him on his special day. We'd wait for a better day – a day when he was more alert so he could enjoy celebrating. As I gazed on his resting body, swathed from head to toe in white bandages, tears streamed down my face. This was no way for a teenager to celebrate his birthday!

Holding hands and standing next to Chad's bed, Rocky and I sang quietly. Several times that day we had wished him happy birthday and reminded him that today, June 1, he turned 17 years old.

My mind drifted as we finished the standard refrain. Chad's birthdays always included a family dinner and usually boisterous fun with friends and other family members like grandparents, aunts, uncles, and cousins. This year would have been no exception. We could have eaten anywhere – Pizza Hut, the local truck stop for their fabulous breakfast menu, or the Royal Fork for all the choices on the buffet line. On the weekend, his friends would have come to our house to celebrate. I could picture it all in my mind: Chad laughingly blowing out candles while his friends and family crowded around the table at our home. Chad gobbling pizza, guzzling Diet Coke, clowning around with his friends. Seeing him in the hospital, I shook my head. *This isn't fair! It isn't right!*

Memories of other birthdays crowded into my head. When he was in elementary school, we usually took a group of five or six boys to a local fast-food restaurant for hamburgers and then it was either bowling, swimming at a local hotel, or a movie.

Sometimes, Chad preferred to celebrate at home with lots of friends and relatives surrounding him. It was equally important for him to include time with our family and his friends on his special day. With a June 1 birthday, we always planned an outdoor barbecue with massive amounts of hamburgers, chips, pickles, and cake. We hoped for a warm, dry day, but whatever the weather, it was always a hilarious time with as many as 20 people whooping it up, eating, and playing basketball, badminton or volleyball with us.

One year, I put trick candles on Chad's cake. We had so much fun watching Chad blow and blow, only to have them re-light. He and his friends were delighted with the surprise and soon everyone was trying to blow them out, clowning around and laughing hysterically! Of course, gifts were the most important part of the celebration. Chad wasn't impressed with clothes, so we made sure to wrap up several toys. One year, it was a new bicycle. In more recent years he received a stereo, cassette tapes, a Nintendo and games, packages of baseball cards, a baseball glove, and jerseys or jackets with the official logos of the Braves and Steelers.

Five days after Chad's birthday, the doctors removed the halo, which considerably lifted my spirits. Even if his condition wasn't much improved, from a mother's standpoint he sure looked better!

Later that same day, as the therapist worked to stretch Chad's legs, a tendon in his right knee tore. To heal, his knee would be immobilized for four to six weeks. That meant no therapy on that knee – another set back. It also delayed progress toward getting him back on his feet. I wondered if the roller coaster would ever slow down and let us off!

By the middle of June, the doctors decided that the skin grafts on Chad's face had healed, and surgically removed the staples holding the skin together. That meant the beginning of a new phase of Chad's recovery: wearing the plastic face mask to improve his appearance and support the healing tissues.

We met an occupational therapist named Angela, who told us the face mask technique was actually developed in the 1970s by

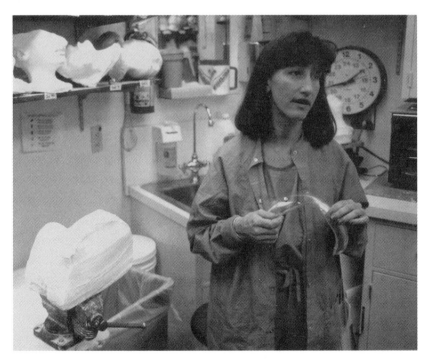

Angela, an occupational therapist, explains the function of the face mask.

another therapist at the burn center. St. Paul-Ramsey pioneered the treatment that is now a standard for burn patients across the world. Angela explained that the mask, which staff called a transparent splint, would compress scar tissue against the muscles and bones in Chad's face, reconstructing it to look somewhat like his face before the accident. It would also flatten some of the rigid scars, called hypertrophic scarring, and decrease pain, sensitivity and itchiness.

First, the staff had to make a negative impression of Chad's face. He reclined in a chair, with his hairline and eyes covered by petroleum jelly. Then, a lukewarm, plaster-type mixture like that used in making dental impressions was spooned and smoothed over his face. Fast-setting plaster strips were placed over the impression, which resembled floppy Jell-O. After about 30 minutes, Chad was told to sit up, take a deep breath and puff out his cheeks to break the seal. The resulting impression was gently removed, yielding the negative impression from which they made a plaster cast.

The plastic splint, made from snowmobile windshield plastic heated for molding, was formed on the plaster cast. It would take many revisions before it fit precisely. That didn't mean that it would ever be comfortable; but through the mask, the underlying scars would appear pale instead of angry red. As Chad's facial swelling decreased, the mask was continually revised, sometimes daily, and soon therapists devised a night mask for him to wear while sleeping. The day mask permitted clear vision and speech while the night mask fit his more relaxed skin while lying down, protected his eyes, and accommodated a mouth splint.

As with every other step toward recovery, the face mask came with requirements: rigorous facial exercises and medication to handle the pain and itching. Chad gradually adjusted to this new therapy, although resisting at first. He wore the mask for just a few hours a day and slowly worked up to virtually 24 hours a day, except when bathing or eating. He couldn't be without the mask for more than an hour at a time, and the therapists predicted he'd wear it for up to 18 months. The goal was for Chad's new skin to be flat and soft, the proper color, durable, and with the least possible wrinkling.

Since it was summer and the school term had ended, many of Chad's friends and their parents visited. For Chad, this was a real turning point in his emotional recovery because his friends reinforced their written messages from the previous months. They visibly cared about him and that face-to-face encouragement helped spur an improved attitude.

Amid newfound joy and optimism, Chad contracted pneumonia in late June. It not only affected his breathing, but it also made his blood pressure skyrocket. His heart raced and the staff worked diligently to control it. For three days, Chad and the medical team fought pneumonia's effect on his heart while Rocky and I haunted the burn center day and night. Keeping vigil, we prayed for God to work through the medical staff to help our son through this new trauma, and for Him to ease our worries as the roller coaster took a new turn. We only left the hospital for short periods of time to clean up at the hotel.

Once again, we listened as the ventilator hissed in Chad's room. His damaged lungs, already struggling to heal from the fire's effects, needed extra help to supply oxygen, so vital to the healing process. After several days, his heart rate and blood pressure returned to normal, although he'd fight the pneumonia for six more weeks. Until he won this battle, we couldn't relax. We lived day to day, waiting for the next crisis or milestone.

CHAPTER TEN

One Giant Step

As CHAD'S CONDITION SLOWLY IMPROVED, winter's unre-
lenting, icy grip was released and temperate air returned to
the upper Midwest. The snow melted, and during our daily two-
block walk from our hotel to the hospital we noticed beautiful,
bright green grass overtaking the drab, brown colors on the hilly
streets near the hospital. Blooming flowers lined walkways and
smiled from the large planters at the hospital's main entrance. As the
outdoors warmed, summer breezed into the Twin Cities.

With all the signs of new life in God's creation, I began to feel
more confident about Chad and our family's future. A hotel suite
had been our home base since February 27, and I found my
thoughts turning more often to home, to our friends and neighbors,
to our life there. But, because the train accident and resulting fire
had destroyed our home and everything we owned, I couldn't picture a house that I could call "home." We had come so far in the
past five months, I allowed myself to think about my dream of
bringing Chad home.

On July 27, Chad reached 90 degrees on the tilt table. The
next day, Ray and Wayne, two burly orderlies, held Chad firmly in
his upright position as they unstrapped him from the board.

Pain flashed across Chad's face and tears streamed down his face as he stood on his own two feet for the first time in five months. It was excruciating and Chad moaned loudly. Rocky and I held our breath as we watched with helpless empathy from across the room. As Ray and Wayne set Chad's feet on the floor, they told him today's goal was walking one or two steps, then he could sit in a chair they'd placed directly behind him.

I held a camera for Chad's first steps in five months. The room was so charged with emotional expectation, I could barely see my son through my tears.

"Okay, Chad. It's time to take those first steps. Just take a couple of steps and we'll set you back in the chair," Ray said as he closely watched Chad's face to see if Chad understood his directions.

Not surprisingly, Chad wouldn't do what Ray asked. He didn't take one or two steps. As he haltingly shuffled one foot in front of the other, he took three steps forward, then turned around and took the same number of steps back to the chair. Exhausted and overtaken by pain, he sank into the chair, but not before I saw the pride shining in his eyes. And he saw it reflected in our eyes and those of the orderlies and nurses. Tears flowed freely from everyone in the room that day.

"You know, success on the football field and the basketball court is nothing compared with this. It's nothing. This is success," said Wayne, wiping the tears after he made sure Chad was comfortably situated. Wayne understood Chad's ordeal and our pride from a parent's perspective. His daughter had suffered from a full body burn like Chad's when she was a child, and she had recovered.

As I captured Chad's biggest milestone yet on film, I sent up a joyful prayer of thanks from my heart. I thanked God once again for Chad's determination to do things his way. Chad had shown all of us that he would overcome the burns that had devastated his youthful frame. Now, nothing could hold him back. He was on the way to reclaiming his life. Hallelujah!

A few weeks before taking his first steps, Chad began seeing one of the hospital's psychologists on the recommendation of Chad's medical team. Like us, they worried about his apparent lack of response to the accident and resulting injuries. Chad wasn't at all receptive to counseling. He usually refused to communicate with the therapist, who did most of the talking. We wanted Chad to cooperate with him but, knowing Chad as Rocky and I did, we weren't at all surprised when the sessions didn't go well. Despite knowing that he'd deal with things in his own way, we felt the sessions helped Chad, who listened and mentally filed information for later reflection. Chad saw the psychologist weekly or every two weeks for about three months, then Chad ended the sessions.

Throughout the summer, Chad's recovery steadily continued. He walked more and more – first, just around the circular nurses' station, then down the hall, then to the cafeteria or therapy sessions. We pushed the wheelchair along and Chad would usually ride part of the way. As his endurance increased, he used the chair less often. With his increased activities came solid food: pizza, pizza, and more sausage and cheese pizza, strawberries, peanut butter toast, nachos – all his favorites. His IV, which had sustained his body, was disconnected.

On the last day of July, Chad donned his favorite Atlanta Braves ball cap and a pair of sunglasses borrowed from a staff member. He snuggled into a recliner with wheels and we rolled him down the hall and into the elevator. We descended the five flights to the main lobby and took him outside for the first time since he arrived at Ramsey.

Aside from the nurse who accompanied us, it was the first time the four of us had been together outside the hospital since the accident five months earlier. We needed to protect Chad, who was still wearing his hospital gown over pressure bandages, from the bright light. He was used to subdued lighting in his hospital room. We draped a blanket over his lap and legs, taking care to cover as much of his skin as possible.

The trip outdoors lasted just 45 minutes, but Chad reveled in it! Hearing the birds, seeing flowers, and feeling a fresh breeze helped Chad realize there was more to life than his daily hospital routine. He breathed deeply, and his upturned face shone with pure joy, like a child discovering a butterfly for the first time. As if to reinforce the importance of this milestone, a week later the medical staff upgraded Chad's condition to fair – a major development for our family. In celebration, the staff allowed Chad to stay up late and let us stay later than usual to watch an evening baseball game. We topped off the celebration with what else? pizza!

During the next few days, we began a new therapy that was more appealing for Chad because it drew on his baseball and basketball skills honed over years of practice. It was also extremely important to his recovery. In his left hand, he'd hold a red Nerf-type ball, imprinted with the Cleveland Indians logo, squeeze it, and throw it to one of us. It helped increase the strength in his hand and stretch his arm while keying in on actions familiar to Chad since he'd been throwing a ball since he was about two years old.

A few weeks later, "No Fear," "Keep Improving Chad" and other messages of support flashed across the scoreboard at a professional baseball game in St. Paul. With Chad watching the action on television from his hospital room, Rocky threw out the ceremonial first pitch as the St. Paul Saints faced the Duluth-Superior Dukes. St. Paul fire fighters sponsored the event to raise funds for the new burn center under construction at Ramsey.

Unaffected by the passage of time, the messages of support kept coming. Outside of our immediate family, no one knew the importance of those special remembrances. I know God had a hand in it all, and I know they helped speed Chad's recovery.

Before Scott left one weekend, he presented his brother with an autographed poster from the country music group, Little Texas. Chad's favorite band, the musicians had recently played at the North Dakota State Fair in Minot. Their well-wishes helped encourage Chad, who grinned with pleasure when Scott showed him the poster. The poster also helped Chad connect with happenings back home. He and his friends usually made at least one trip to the Midway.

Home. A word that brought both comfort and uncertainty.

I worried about where we would live and how we could care for Chad, even though we didn't know what kind of care he'd need after leaving the hospital. Rocky eased my fears by sharing his plans for our family's new life together.

Sitting aimlessly for all those months in nondescript hospital waiting rooms, Rocky had drawn our dream home in his mind. It would be open, light, and airy, with a two-bedroom apartment and garage for Chad and Scott at one end. While he would need our help for years to come, Chad was becoming an adult and would want some privacy.

Some of the months of worry that lined Rocky's face would lift when he talked about our new home. He drew on his carpentry skills, designing a single-level dwelling with a gently sloping driveway and front yard. A hill just right for climbing was behind the house. It would be air conditioned, with large bedrooms to accommodate the special bed Chad would likely need when he first came home. In late summer, the contractors began moving dirt, and we were more eager than ever to return to Burlington where all four of us could return to normal lives.

Normal. What's that, I wondered? Our ordinary lives had been turned upside down in a flash and I knew I'd never again take anything for granted. The nightmares, the memories, the flashbacks would likely be with us for months and, possibly, years to come. We hoped a supportive group of friends would help Chad readjust.

Now, with a picture in our minds, we were drawing a blueprint for our new lives. Overlooking the scenic Souris River valley about two miles northwest of Burlington, the home would be an answer to my prayers for permanency. It would give us a fresh start in many ways, and it wouldn't bring any grim reminders of our all too recent nightmare.

We couldn't hear or see any trains from there.

CHAPTER ELEVEN

Do It Your Way

ONE EVENING AS CHAD, ROCKY, AND I sat outside the hospital, an airplane zoomed over us. Chad turned his head and looked up – he hadn't heard an airplane for months. We sat quietly and soon a small, brown sparrow hopped along the bench next to Chad. The week before, Chad had been delighted with his first ride in a vehicle, our new teal-colored van. After the dramatic turn Chad's life had taken, he wasn't taking anything for granted any more.

I reflected on the past few months, which now blurred together in a monotonous, repetitive scene – therapy, tutoring, therapy, tutoring, therapy, therapy, therapy. Chad had to accomplish certain goals set by his doctors before they would consider letting him return home.

His days began at sunrise with lessons in dressing and brushing his teeth. Definitely not a morning person, Chad resisted the routine that clashed with his desire to sleep. Frustrations became commonplace. Daily tasks that almost everyone accomplishes without thinking were nearly insurmountable obstacles. Making a sandwich or microwave popcorn could reduce Chad to tears. One day, in the safety of his room, he placed his gloved hand over his eyes as an anguished sob burst from his soul. Tears cascaded down his face as I knelt next to him in his wheelchair.

It had been a frustrating Monday. Out of sorts since waking, Chad's stretches had been painful. His experience with the microwave failed because he lacked enough strength to push the buttons, and the therapists wanted him to pedal the stationary bike forward instead of backward. After a weekend of visitors and a trip to our motel room, he tired easily and had minimal patience.

"It's okay, son," I said, gently stroking his left shoulder. I reminded him that releasing all of those emotions, building up throughout the day, was as important to his recovery as all of the therapy. As I knelt beside him, I silently prayed for God to carry him through this difficult time. Chad needed to trust God, and to let Him help.

Slowly, Chad nodded. I could feel God's loving arms encircling us as a feeling of calm permeated the hospital room. I lightly clasped his hand and thanked God for saving Chad's life. I asked Him to continue helping Chad through his daily struggle to regain his independence.

By late August, Chad was walking outside his room and all around the burn unit, to and from his bath, and to physical therapy with some help from a wheelchair. Being ambulatory, Chad needed real clothes to replace his hospital gowns. I joyfully shopped for an assortment of brightly colored "cool" trunks to go with his Atlanta Braves jerseys and caps sent by his friends.

Our days at the hospital continued with peaks and valleys — some disappointments, but more and more days of marked progress. Chad had been receiving twice-daily injections of Heparin, a blood-thinner to prevent blood clots. Each morning, and each night after we left, the nurses gave Chad the painful shot that often brought tears because the medicine burned as it flowed into his body. Chad hated for us to leave because he knew it was time for the shot. At times, he begged the nurses to skip the injection.

On Friday, September 2, Chad's doctors, who wanted him to push himself even harder walking, made a deal with him. If Chad would walk three laps around the circular nurses' station three times a day, he could discontinue the Heparin. Seconds later, Chad was out of bed and heading toward the desk, eager to hold up his end of the bargain. He continued the ritual until the time he was transferred from the burn unit. There was no way he'd endure the injections again.

In early September, the doctors upgraded Chad's condition from fair to stable. That signaled another ray of hope for us, and although the doctors didn't give us any idea when Chad could be released, I secretly hoped he could be home by the end of November.

Chad made quick progress once he recovered from his bout with pneumonia and began walking on his own, although he was still fighting the staph infection and wore a surgical-like mask as he moved to various treatment sites in the hospital.

I rejoiced the day he mastered a firm grip on a red, wooden peg, using the long pale fingers of his only arm, and jumped a peg in an adjacent hole on a game board. He delighted in slam-dunking his Nerf ball for newspaper photographers and challenged nearly everyone to a hoop shoot or a game of horse. He no longer wore the usual hospital gowns; instead, he often dressed in an Atlanta Braves shirt and red plaid trunks, his long legs and arm swathed in protective Ace bandages with white Nike tennis shoes on his feet.

When he wasn't playing ball, his left arm was raised in a sling to keep the skin stretched and the swelling minimal. His light brown hair covered most of his head, yet we could still see evidence of the fire's fury – no ear lobes, no tip to his nose, his eyes peering through reddened slits where they were again sewn shut to stretch his eyelids. His face was distorted behind the stiff plastic mask. Yet despite his appearance, Chad was healing quickly, thanks to a legion of talented staff who worked tirelessly in so many ways.

Joyce was one of those extraordinarily talented people. A physical therapist, she was known as "No-Choice Joyce" for her no-nonsense approach to her patients. Someone said if anyone could motivate Chad, it was Joyce. A large, Afro-American woman with closely-cropped hair and small white earrings, she was as compassionate as she was tough.

Even though Chad had much to accomplish, Joyce let him decide which activities to do first. That helped him to feel in control. But Joyce didn't let Chad get by with just maintaining what he'd accomplished the previous day. If he had completed three or four repetitions one day, the next day she would expect five or six.

'No-choice' Joyce, one of Chad's nurses at Ramsey Burn Center, stands encircled by Chad, Scott and Rocky.

With Joyce's coaching, Chad stretched his knee ligaments and took his first steps up stairs and back down again.

Through leg lifts and buttocks thrusts, Joyce commanded Chad to "scoot your buns over to the edge. Twist your buns a little bit. All right. Hamstring-stretch extraordinaire!" She held the stump where his right arm had been, told him to lift it and directed him to "push, push, push."

When Chad told her he was hot from the exertion, she waved her hands over his face, bringing a slight cooling breeze. She knew his new skin couldn't sweat, and the only way for his body to cool itself was through his head and arm pits.

"We have to do these exercises or you don't have a snowball's chance in hell of getting a prosthesis. It's your choice," she said. Turning slightly away from Chad, she glanced at the clock, wiped a sympathetic look from her face and replaced it with a cheery smile.

"Guess what? It's time to go. How time flies when you're having fun," she said, laughingly.

Chad laughed too, even though the sessions tired him and were followed by Cliff's tutoring. The two were studying U.S. history, Cliff reading the textbook assignment aloud to Chad. Cliff was just the right mix for Chad – pushing him to learn, remember and excel in his studies while using his insight to meet Chad's unique needs. Tender and caring, he was personally concerned about Chad, far beyond the usual teacher-pupil relationship. One day, their discussions turned to computers and how a computer would aid Chad's school work. A few days later, Cliff brought a computer from his office and set it up in Chad's room. The arrival of the machine led to a new goal. Chad wanted to play Nintendo again, and to play it well.

One of Chad's therapists took measurements of his fingers and called the Nintendo company, which at no charge made a special controller with custom-made buttons to fit his left hand. The day it arrived at the hospital, the therapist set it up and Chad began playing immediately. It was important therapy for Chad. First, his hand and finger dexterity improved quickly and second, Chad enjoyed it so much that he played every chance he had.

I could see the light at the end of our tunnel growing larger with each milestone Chad reached; it wouldn't be long before the hospital was a mere memory.

CHAPTER TWELVE

Together Again

TOWARD THE END OF SEPTEMBER, St. Paul-Ramsey opened its new, $6.4 million burn center. Constructed on the north roof of the hospital's main building, the 18,000-square-foot addition almost doubled the size of the current unit and was designed for 18 patients, two more than the current area, with mostly private rooms. It featured two overnight sleeping rooms for families, individual temperature controls in intensive care, and bedside computers. Artwork decorated some of the ceilings in an effort to distract patients from their situations. Compared to the area where Chad was now living, the new center was a palace! His staph infection was cured and shortly before the new wing opened, Chad and I toured it. He would be the first patient, and was allowed to select his new room. He chose one with a stunning, sunny view of downtown St. Paul.

Our excitement at moving to the new burn center was short-lived as the doctors announced they were transferring Chad to the rehabilitation unit. It was real progress and a dream come true! Like the burn unit, the rehabilitation unit bustled with activity and was where what I called "the gettin' home stuff," would happen.

Chad's days were consumed with therapy, learning how to hold objects with his left hand and mastering the art of writing his name. Over and over again he practiced writing, "Yale," which is what his friends called him, and "42," his jersey number. At his request, we often wheeled Chad outside in his chair. Sometimes, he would even walk part of the way.

One Saturday morning, Chad was eager with excitement. Rocky and Scott, who had been home in Burlington for a week, were arriving at the airport. For the first time, Chad would ride along to surprise his dad and brother. Before the accident, Chad was usually cooking up surprises and practical jokes, so I was glad to see his "old-self" enthusiasm returning. We drove to the airport and parked in the usual spot where I'd picked them up for months. Soon, Rocky and Scott stepped through the glass doors and stopped in amazement when they saw Chad. We were all grinning from ear-to-ear.

The next surprise came later that evening. Chad received a dinner pass, which meant he could eat supper with us. He chose Taco Bell. We cruised through the drive-up lane, ordered our food and ate in the van in the parking lot. Everything seemed perfect; our family was together again. Then Chad spilled his taco meat, leaving a greasy stain on the carpet. We laughed; everything was just like old times. The spot stayed there, a reminder of our perfect day.

During his stay at the hospital, Chad had met Dave Davis, a good-hearted sports enthusiast. Dave and Chad immediately formed a bond based on sports. We knew Dave and his wife, RayAnn, would become fast family friends.

A hospital employee, Dave often visited desperately ill youngsters who told him about their heroes, most of them sports athletes. He had established the "Support Thru Sports" program in 1991, procuring baseball, hockey and golf memorabilia like autographed posters and clothing for the kids. He had been amazed to see the impact it made on their physical recoveries.

At the urging of patients and their families, the hospital had built a large cabinet dedicated to the program. Dave had expanded it to include nearly every sport imaginable, and photos of hospital visits to sick children by key players from teams across the United States were displayed there. In the new burn unit, Dave's five-by-nine-foot cabinet showcases his personal sports collection with about one-third of it dedicated to Chad's accident, recovery, and relationship with Greg Olson.

Soon after meeting Dave, we arranged an October 4 press conference to let people know about Chad's progress. Chad was excited for the interview because he had messages to send to his friends and family back home. What he didn't know was that Dave had arranged for Greg Olson, one of Chad's heroes from the Atlanta Braves, to appear in person to surprise Chad.

Rocky, Scott, and I knew what was about to happen and we could hardly restrain ourselves. After a full day of therapy, Chad returned to his room where television cameras and reporters waited. Dave, who had become a close friend, came into the room, too. And then, Greg Olson walked in.

Greg had been a catcher for the Atlanta Braves for many years and was coaching a minor league team, the Minneapolis Loons. Dave introduced Greg to Chad, who was speechless with surprise and excitement. Then Dave gave Chad a signed, numbered lithograph of Dale Murphy who, in Chad's eyes, was the ultimate Braves player. Greg gave him a Loons T-shirt, a picture of himself during his days with the Braves, and a bat on which he had inscribed, "To Chad: Before long I want to see you swinging this bat, Greg Olson."

Television cameras rolled, capturing this very special moment for Chad. He answered a few of the reporters' questions, yet still seemed in awe of his new-found sports friends. The reporters wanted to know what Chad remembered about the accident that brought him to Ramsey. Composed despite his astonishment, he didn't hesitate and told them.

"I ran out of my room and looked out the door. I could see one of the cars of the train lying in our yard. We decided we'd better get some lights on over there because it was so dark. So I got dressed and I went outside to start my car and go over there. I unplugged the engine heater and that's about the last thing I really remember."

As Chad told his story for the first time, I marveled at how far he had come in his recovery. Then I looked at Greg Olson, who was wiping away tears.

After the media left, Greg asked Chad if he could visit him again, sometime when just the two of them could be alone to talk baseball together. I was amazed that Greg seemed to shun his notoriety, and genuinely seemed concerned about visiting with Chad away from his usual limelight. Chad simply smiled and said he'd like that a lot.

I didn't know if Greg would really return, although I was hoping so. The next day I called to thank him for visiting Chad, but he wasn't home. I talked with his wife, Lisa, and asked that she pass along my thanks to Greg. Her comments surprised me.

"Cindy, what you don't know is that Chad motivated Greg. Greg feels very privileged to be a part of Chad's life now. It is important to him," Lisa said.

I was so happy to hear that Chad had helped someone else, even though Greg's visit did far more to encourage Chad than all my talking. Greg visited Chad several more times, and telephoned him every other week. Surrounded by Atlanta Braves' posters in Chad's room, the two talked about their shared interest. Chad always wore a Braves shirt for his visits; the two became baseball soul mates. It was the beginning of a lifelong friendship, and Greg told me one day when he left, that he would always be there for Chad.

Special visitors like Dave and Greg helped Chad think about his future, and see that it was important to set goals for his life. Preparing for discharge, he attended regular meetings where the staff reviewed his progress and told him what they expected of him in the future. He set goals to accomplish before leaving the hospital, and the staff estimated the time it would take for him to achieve those goals. Chad would ultimately be responsible for setting his discharge date.

At a meeting in early October, Chad set November 19 as his release date. The staff agreed, telling him it was realistic given what he aimed to accomplish before leaving. He'd already exceeded his physical therapy goals with Joyce, but needed to master dressing himself, improving his writing skills, brushing his teeth, and combing his hair. To show he'd built up his endurance, he must be able to climb a full flight of stairs.

In addition to the in-hospital successes, he wanted to graduate from high school, drive his own car, and get a job so he could be a productive person. They were good goals, and easy things to think about.

In the meantime, Chad visited an eye specialist and was fitted with new glasses. Before the accident he wore contacts, but we knew that would have to wait.

Preparing for full discharge, the doctors allowed Chad to live with us at the hotel two blocks away. We moved to a larger suite, with connecting rooms and a large bedroom that could accommodate the hospital bed for Chad and a regular bed for Scott. Even though he was living in the hotel with us, Chad continued his weekly hospital regimen – six days of therapy and five days of tutoring, beginning at 8 a.m. and ending at about 5 p.m. Most days, Chad just couldn't get going and we were late for his first appointments.

With Chad's increased endurance and mobility, and November 19 moving closer, wonderful things began happening. Chad and I were guests at a Minnesota Timberwolves-Chicago Bulls game, when the Bulls, including Scottie Pippin and the others, invited Chad to sit on the bench with them during warm-ups! It was a thrill for us both; Chad's only disappointment was that Michael Jordan wasn't playing with them at the time.

Another time, our family was given a private box at a Minnesota Vikings game. Chad's cousin, Shawn, is a huge Vikings fan, so we asked him to join us. Although the Pittsburgh Steelers were Chad's favorite football team, he thoroughly enjoyed the game and the unique privilege of seeing it from a private box.

Chad, Scott and cousin Shawn enjoy a football game at the Minneapolis Metrodome.

The CBS television show "This Morning" heard about Chad's story and sent a film crew to some of his therapy sessions and did an interview with Chad and the rest us at the hospital. Chad was prepared to answer their questions, and he handled the media attention with an offhanded indifference. Rocky and I were excited about Chad's story being broadcast to millions of people because it gave us another opportunity to proclaim God's work, which we viewed as a modern-day miracle.

Not long before his first nationally-televised interview was to air, Chad was surprised by another sports celebrity. Dave Winfield, who was negotiating with the Cleveland Indians, was planning a surprise visit to see Chad. We learned about Dave through another family in the burn center. The mother of another patient, who had family connections to the Winfields, asked if Chad would like to meet Dave. I knew it would be a highlight for him, so she arranged the meeting.

When Dave walked in the door, Chad gasped and stared in amazement. Dave brought an autographed baseball, a picture, and his book, "Dave Winfield – 3,000 and Counting." He autographed it simply, "To Chad, My very best wishes, Dave Winfield, 1994." The sponge ball Chad had been slam-dunking had the Indians' emblem so Dave autographed it, too.

Before Dave left he told Chad, "The next home run I hit, it's for you, buddy." We knew he meant it. Like Greg Olson, he didn't make a big deal of his celebrity status.

Between the celebrity visits and sporting events, we continued to prepare for Chad's departure. The physical therapy director and two nurses from Trinity Medical Center in Minot, where Chad would continue his physical therapy upon discharge, arrived at the hospital to learn about his schedule. They spent an entire day at Ramsey arranging aftercare treatment because after we got home,

Chad's eight-hour routine of physical therapy and tutoring would become their responsibility. The Minot burn rehabilitation team included the hospital's home health, occupational and physical therapy departments, making for a coordinated effort. It was important to Chad's continued recovery that his new medical team continue on the same course begun at Ramsey.

One day away from discharge, November 18, 1994, the burn unit staff held a farewell party for Chad. It was only the second such event they'd ever had, so we felt very special. They invited the media, and several staff members recalled Chad's courage during his lengthy and painful convalescence. It made Rocky and I proud!

"I can truly say that your journey for survival has been nothing short of miraculous and inspiring," said Pastor John, the hospital chaplain who had supported us throughout our stay and became a fast friend.

Dr. Solem, the burn center's director, reminded us how deeply Chad had been burned and how thrilled he was to see him well enough to go home.

Wearing a Chicago Bulls shirt and cap, Chad had entered the room in a wheelchair but later stood at a microphone to answer questions. Asked what he most looked forward to doing at home, Chad quietly said, "Sitting home and watching TV." Of his ordeal, he said he had learned something about himself, that "I'm stronger than I thought."

I had mixed emotions about leaving. Even though I looked forward to going home, I would be leaving behind the hospital staff. They had been my support for the past nine months, the people who had repaired my son's body and helped him regain his strength and abilities. This was a place where we'd made real, enduring friendships, a place where people cared as much as I – as a mother

– cared for my son. I couldn't describe how important these people had become to me. Can you ever adequately thank someone for saving your child's life?

With tears filling my eyes and spilling down my cheeks, I presented the burn unit a plaque with my favorite poem, "Footprints," the story of how Christ carries people through difficult times.

FOOTPRINTS

"One night a man had a dream. He dreamed he was walking along the beach with the Lord. Across the sky flashed scenes from his life. For each scene, he noticed two sets of footprints in the sand: one belonging to him, and the other to the Lord.

When the last scene of his life flashed before him, he looked back at the footprints in the sand. He noticed that many times along the path of his life there was only one set of footprints. He also noticed that it happened at the very lowest and saddest times in his life.

This really bothered him and he questioned the Lord about it. "Lord, you said that once I decided to follow you, you'd walk with me all the way. But I have noticed that during the most troublesome times in my life, there is only one set of footprints. I don't understand why, when I needed you most, you would leave me."

The Lord replied, "My precious child, I love you and I would never leave you. During your times of trial and suffering, when you see only one set of footprints, it was then that I carried you."

– AUTHOR UNKNOWN

I asked them to hang it in the family room in the hopes that other families, forced into the same type of trauma and tragedy, could gain strength from it. We survived our ordeal by having faith in God, sticking together, and facing each day as it came. I wanted to share that hope with others.

The next morning, we checked out of our hotel, signed discharge papers at the hospital and as a family, walked down the steps and out the doors to the van that would take us to the airport. A Minot television station followed the day's events as if filming a documentary. As we entered the Minneapolis airport, Chad walked tall beside his brother. Rocky and I beamed with pride.

CHAPTER THIRTEEN

An Early Thanksgiving

THE 727 JETLINER LANDED AT THE MINOT AIRPORT at 2:35 p.m., one wintery week before Thanksgiving 1994. We had prayed, waited, planned, and hoped for this moment, and it finally had arrived. After 268 days and 20 surgeries, Chad was nearly home. Now, as Scott put it, we'd be a family all the time, not just on weekends.

My heart swelled with pride for my son. From having such slim odds nine months ago, he had progressed from being in a wheelchair to walking on his own now.

On the flight from Minneapolis to Minot, I thought back to all that had happened and choked up. When the television reporter, who accompanied us on the airplane asked me how I felt, my response was, "I'm really flying high today. This is the ultimate."

The other 50 passengers on the flight streamed off the airplane ahead of us, most of them offering their best wishes to Chad and us. Then it was our turn, and we slowly walked up the aisle. Chad needed time to make his way from his seat into the terminal. Faintly we heard chanting and Chad, wearing his plastic face mask, sports jersey, black sweat pants and an Atlanta Braves baseball cap, smiled. His feet seemed to float in his red shoes.

As we approached the airport reception area, we heard the crowd chanting: "Yale, YALE, YALE!" Then, "We want CHAD, we want CHAD!" He was walking ahead of me so I couldn't see his face. I imagined he was grinning eagerly. I was swallowing my tears of joy.

When we rounded the final corner, and saw inside the terminal, the immensity of the crowd surprised us. We knew our friends had planned a welcome home party but this was beyond anything we had imagined. More than 200 people jammed the small waiting area. Everyone was waving yellow ribbons, television and newspaper cameras were everywhere. As soon as they saw Chad, the crowd erupted into deafening screams and applause as hundreds of yellow streamers danced in their hands.

Waving his swathed and splinted arm to the appreciative crowd, Chad quietly said, "I'm glad everybody showed up. It's great!"

Cindy looks on as Grandpa Sonny gives a big, welcome-home hug to Chad.

We were home!

We walked through the double, glass doors and faced a wall of family and friends, each of them smiling, waving, many clutching tissues to catch their tears. Chad's Grandpa Sonny stepped forward and hugged him first. After a brief pause, Chad's five best friends surged forward to envelop him in bear hugs, mindless of the tears streaming down their faces. Signs welcoming us hung everywhere. Suspended from the ceiling hung a huge banner made by the church youth group. Rocky, Scott, and I hung back a bit to let Chad take it all in. At center stage, he smiled through his face mask, swaying slightly, not wanting to let go of the moment.

After several minutes, we made our way to the airport entrance where our van, decorated with a yellow balloon bouquet, waited to take us to a community potluck dinner in our honor. The Ward County sheriff, one of the first people on the scene when the fire engulfed our home in February, led the mile-long caravan of more than 100 decorated, honking cars to the Des Lacs High School gym. During the 10-mile, winding drive we passed banners and posters welcoming us home and hundreds of smiling, waving people lining the highway. On the side of a hill near the high school was a larger-than-life tribute: a huge "42" made by Chad's classmates from white spray-painted rocks.

At the school, hundreds of yellow ribbons tied to tree branches fluttered in the breeze. When we walked into the gym where Chad had played countless basketball games, nearly 400 well-wishers stood and applauded. Several six-foot-long tables lined one wall, straining under the weight of steaming casseroles, salads, boxes of buns and luscious desserts. From a special head table for our family, we looked out at the crowd that included friends, family, rescue workers, fire fighters from three rural departments who extinguished the blaze so many months ago, and people who had prayed for us. Their faces were a blur, and yet they had each played a part in Chad's recovery.

Sharing and caring from their hearts; this was the nicest way possible for us to be welcomed home. Chad's friends gave him a basketball with "42" and "Forever" written on it. My dear friend, Paula, who organized the party, led the crowd in the sweetest thanksgiving prayer I had ever heard.

"Dear Lord, as we gather here today to celebrate this homecoming, we thank you for your many blessings. Most importantly, we thank you for the gift of life you've given to Chad. We know the many prayers sent Your way were heard. Thank you for bringing Chad back to us. Amen."

Then, as folks began making their way to the food-laden tables, Chad's friends rushed to the front, loaded with boxes of sausage and cheese pizza from Pizza Hut. His buddy, Bill, served Chad the first, and largest, piece while the others grabbed seats close by. Smiles ringed the room, cameras flashed. One by one, people came to the table to greet us, to see Chad, to congratulate him. As I took in the scene, I felt overwhelmed and humbled. Right there, I said another prayer of thanksgiving – this time for a caring community.

Chad survived this ordeal, thanks to the God who carried us and carried us and continued to carry us for almost nine months. Now, once again, He was beside us, basking in the glory of the day.

CHAPTER FOURTEEN

A Mother's Dream

T HE STANDING-ROOM-ONLY CROWD broke into rhythmic applause when Chad, one of 47 fresh-faced high school seniors, crossed the stage to accept his hard-won diploma. His red graduation robe swirled around his lanky frame as he walked slowly and steadily toward the podium. A grin strained his grafted cheeks behind the plastic mask.

It was a moment he'd dreamt about – and worked toward – for months. He'd studied with his tutor, Cliff, every day as part of his physical and occupational therapy at Ramsey. And he studied in the car between school and physical therapy sessions at Trinity Medical Center in Minot. Never one to log many study hours before the accident, Chad surprised us by earning high marks, good enough to make the honor roll for the first time in his life. Despite missing half his junior year and much of his senior year, Chad was graduating with his class!

As tears streamed down my face, I freeze-framed the moment and tucked it into my heart. I'd relive Chad's achievement many times in the future. High school graduation was a milestone that 15 months ago was a goal, not a certainty. And as the applause and cheers filled the Des Lacs gym, I sent a prayer of thanksgiving once again to God.

Greg Olson, Chad's dear friend, delivered the commencement address. The retired catcher had met U. S. presidents, country music stars, and rap singers. Until May 19, 1994, he had refused invitations to speak at high school graduations but he made an exception because he wanted to see for himself what was so special about Chad's classmates. His speech held a simple message relevant to Chad's nine-month struggle to live: a positive attitude holds the key to success in life.

Chad and his best friend, Bill, graduate together from Des Lacs-Burlington High School in 1995.

Days before graduation, Chad granted several interview requests from television and newspaper reporters. He tired of the attention, but his answers never changed.

"I don't really think about it that much, I guess," he said of the accident. "Sure, I think, well, geez, I wish I never would have gone out there."

While his life was forever changed, Chad was determined to get on with life. He said he always knew things would get better – giving up never crossed his mind – so he gradually learned to accept what he needed to do. Rejoining his loyal friends at graduation spurred him to study, and passing his driving test proved he could attain any goal he set. The day before graduation, he roared home in his shiny-new, black Ford Explorer.

When asked what he'd say to another teen facing a similar, seemingly insurmountable challenge, Chad hesitated only a second, then replied, "Keep fighting. It will get better."

During media interviews, Chad revealed his future plans, which no longer included his previous dream of becoming a sports commentator. He also postponed college, where he planned to study business, until his handwriting improved and he could type faster on his lap top computer.

Instead, he would build a unique sports complex in Minot, the center of a region which opened its heart and its pocketbook to our family.

While the accident robbed him of his life's delight – playing sports – Chad vowed to remain a contender. His Sports World Stadium would look, on the outside, like a real sports stadium with goal-post lighting in the parking lot, a score board and flashing lights. Inside the two-story, 40,000-square foot building, patrons would find a licensed, brand-name sports apparel store, a bar and restaurant called The Dugout, a half-court basketball area, batting cage, and sports arcade.

The ground breaking would be Chad's victory, a symbolic gesture that showed he'd begun a new life.

"I just thought about it one day during physical therapy, and I thought it's something I could do," Chad told reporters. "I'd really like to get going on it this summer. And it's something I can do for the rest of my life."

Before construction could begin, Chad had an important date with the Atlanta Braves. The accident forced him to cancel plans to visit Atlanta for the National Lutheran Youth Gathering, where he'd planned to take in his dream team's action. In June 1995, accompanied by his best friend, Bill, our entire family lived Chad's dream of seeing the Braves play – and win – in person.

On September 22, Chad returned to Ramsey for his 21st surgery, a two-week stay to graft skin on his legs. When he left the hospital, he needed to return every other week for follow up care, then taper off to less-frequent visits over time. Chad's total medical expenses now approached $3 million.

Later that year, Greg Olson sent our family tickets to three World Series games with the Atlanta Braves facing the Cleveland Indians. In October, as guests of the Atlanta Braves, we attended games three, four, and five in Cleveland, Ohio. Chad talked with Greg, who was doing a radio broadcast, and lived his dream of watching his dream team win the ultimate sporting event. The Braves won games one and two in Atlanta; lost game three, won game four and lost game five in Cleveland; and won game six at home in Atlanta to take the 1995 World Series.

Besides boosting the Minot area's economic base by opening a new store, Chad wanted to show his appreciation to the high school students who had sent cards, videos, and gifts – even dedicated their 1994 homecoming festivities to him.

The gym floor where Chad's team practiced and played was long past its prime. Since the Des Lacs High School team practiced and played in the Burlington Elementary School gym, he bought a natural-colored wood floor with the Lakers' logo at center court and on the end lines. It included special installation by a Seattle, Washington, company.

Chad participates in a dedication of the gymnasium floor he purchased for Des Lacs-Burlington High School in 1995.

In April 1996, Chad visited a Minneapolis plastic surgeon, Dr. Allen Van Beek, who discussed the possibilities available through reconstructive surgery. With the face mask no longer needed, Chad would prioritize operations to rebuild his nose and lips, open his mouth, release his neck, and rebuild the end of his thumb and his two curved fingers. He'd need to decide about a prosthetic arm and either rebuild his ears or use prostheses. Chad had developed a herniated stomach the size of a basketball where scar tissue had pushed through the tender linings. The fire destroyed his abdominal muscle tissue, so more surgery was likely. Chad overcame tremendous odds, but will continue to fight health problems for the rest of his life.

My days at home revolved around preparing meals, Chad's daily bedding changes and laundry, and monitoring Chad's heart medications and vitamins. Slowly, I returned to my involvement with the church youth group and was elected president of the church council.

After Chad's graduation, Rocky reopened his carpet cleaning business. Scott returned to college, but lived with Chad in the apartment attached to our home. We struggled to live a "normal" life, but our lives would never be the same.

While we instinctively tried to protect him, Chad's independence pushed us away. He'd jump into his Ford Explorer for daily drives into Minot for physical therapy and wouldn't miss the high school's basketball games. I admired the way he nonchalantly faced the public and the reality of his injuries, a credit to the friends who took him to a college basketball game the day after our welcome home party. They refused to allow Chad to become a recluse, taking him out for pizza, to hang out at the mall, to the movies – treating him the same as they had for years.

As one girl in his class said, "It's the same Chad, just in a different package." He retained his stubborn, strong-willed personality. The only difference I saw was that Chad now loved to read for hours, while he'd barely crack a book before the accident. He still likes to sleep late in the mornings and still prefers his friends' company. He's still stubborn, and he still makes me mad. And, I still love him.

Daily, I fight my anger and frustration at the accidental, unplanned turn our family's life took that wintery morning in 1994. My anger is often directed at the company responsible for the accident that changed our lives forever while its executives are able to go about their normal, daily lives.

I can't forget that Chad balanced on the edge of life and death for months, that we were ripped away from our community of supportive friends and family. We lost our business, our possessions, everything we had worked for.

But more than our material possessions, Chad lost infinitely more. For the rest of his life, he'll be sidelined from the game of life, forced to sit in the shade and watch his friends play baseball rather than joining them, avoiding his senior prom with its handsome young couples laughing and dancing. Fears for his future tear at my heart and I wonder if he is to be robbed of the joys of a loving wife and children. We did nothing to deserve our situation, yet we live with the stares, the whispered rumors, the folks who avoid Chad because of his appearance.

My solace comes from God, who soothes my troubled soul with His comforting words: "I am with you always." I know that He'll continue His care for our family, particularly Chad, as we encounter daily obstacles.

I thank God that He spared my child's life, and I look forward to what He has planned for him. I know God isn't yet through with Chad, and I continue to give his care over to our heavenly Father.

From his birth, my prayer for Chad was that he be whatever he wanted to be, and to be the best he could be at that. It still is my prayer.

Epilogue

O N FEBRUARY 27, 1994, 26 cars of a 59-car Canadian Pacific Railway train derailed 200 feet from the Burlington, North Dakota home of Rocky, Cindy, Scott, and Chad Yale. Fuel or fumes from a ruptured 30,000-gallon butane tanker ignited about the time that Chad Yale, then 16, unplugged the block heater on his car's engine.

The charred remains of the Yale home in Burlington, North Dakota.

The explosion forced the evacuation of 1,200 people in near-by Burlington, and the Yale home burned. A railroad investigation determined the accident was caused by a broken joint bar that held two sections of rail together.

Chad, who nearly perished from third-degree burns to more than 80 percent of his body, lost his right arm, sensation, hair follicles, sweat glands, blood vessels, nerve endings, and muscle tissue over almost all of his body. The fire damaged his heart and kidneys, and impaired the range of motion in his head, neck, back, trunk, hips, legs and feet. It took him almost nine months to recover enough to leave the St. Paul-Ramsey Burn Center.

In December 1995, the Yales sued the railroad for Chad's injuries, suffering, and loss of future income because negotiations

In 1997, Chad became the majority owner of the Austin, MN, Southern Minny Stars; pictured here with Joe Garagiola, Dave Davis and Greg Olson. (Former Atlanta Braves catcher and part owner/manager of Southern Minny Stars.)

with the company had reached a standstill. In July 1996, they reached an out-of-court settlement with CP Rail System for an undisclosed sum. The federal district court sealed the details.

In January 1997, Chad, 19, bought the majority stock in the Southern Minny Stars baseball team, making him the youngest owner of any professional sports franchise. The purchase fulfilled one of Chad's longtime dreams – owning a sports team. The other owners – Greg Olson, Steve Avery, John Smoltz and Greg Maddux – were all either current or former Atlanta Braves team members, and among Chad's sports heroes.

In May 1997, Chad held a groundbreaking ceremony for Sports World Stadium, then returned to Minneapolis the following month where Dr. Allen Van Beek performed Chad's 22nd surgery to correct a herniated stomach and open his constricted mouth. Chad was hospitalized for a month. He now faces one more surgery to finish correcting his stomach. Any other surgeries will be elective and done at Chad's discretion.

Sports World Stadium opened in October 1997 in Minot, North Dakota. Chad, president, and Scott, vice president, both work Monday through Friday at the store. They work with their management staff on day-to-day operations, set long-term goals and plan marketing efforts. They also schedule sporting events like three-on-three basketball tournaments, sand volleyball and adult and youth basketball leagues.

Chad spends time every day with his friends. They watch television sports channels, go to movies and consume massive amounts of pizza. Bill and Chad remain best friends, spending time together just about every day. Chad has traveled to Pittsburgh to watch the Steelers play football, to Atlanta for Brave's baseball, and to Austin, Minnesota to watch his baseball team, the Southern Minny Stars.

While in Minnesota, Chad often visits with friends like Greg Olson and Gene Larkin.

An avid sports fan, he's always on the lookout for a baseball or basketball game to watch.

The Yales pose in 1997 for a family photo at Sports World Stadium, the family entertainment sports mall Chad envisioned and built in Minot.

A restaurant, sports bar, arcade, basketball court and The Athlete's Foot retail store are all under one roof at Sports World Stadium, owned and operated by the Yales.

About the Author

Cindy Yale is living her dream. A rewarding marriage, seeing and working with her adult sons every day, good health, strong friendships, extended family relationships, and a job she loves make her life full and rewarding.

She and Rocky enjoy the new home they built near Burlington. Cindy spends the greater part of her week days 10 miles away at Sports World Stadium, the family sports entertainment mall the Yales opened in Minot in 1997.

Sports World Stadium, an impressive, modernistic, two-story facility with a restaurant, sports bar, retail store, basketball court, batting cage, arcade, and corporate offices, stands as a testament to Chad's desire to give back to the community that supported the Yales through their trials.

Neither this facility nor the new home would exist today had it not been for the trauma that forever changed the Yales' lives. Yet Cindy would give up the home and family business without hesitation if she could turn back the hands of time.

The journey that began five years ago has been bittersweet. Chad's adjustments to life as a handicapped person, their contentious battle with the railroad, Cindy's personal pain caused by lack of understanding from the community that had upheld them during their crisis, and the trials that accompany any new business further battered the Yales at times, yet they emerged united.

Writing the book helped Cindy heal, and fulfilled a promise she had made to God to tell their story and hopefully help someone else through a traumatic situation. She still struggles with anger over what she sees as the railroad's apparent disregard of track maintenance. And while she is intensely proud of Chad's progress, her heart wrenches thinking of the things he will never be able to do and the sports he will never play because of his injuries.

But those are the fleeting moments. Pragmatic and logical by nature, Cindy keeps those regrets to a minimum and concentrates on the present.

"I don't live in the past or the future," she reflected. "Today is a present from God. I plan for tomorrow. I have dreams and goals, but I live for today and little things in life that used to bother me don't nearly as much as they did in the past. I love life now."

Much of life now revolves around Sports World Stadium where Cindy has immersed herself in her job as general manager. Chad is Chief Executive Officer, Scott Vice President, and Rocky oversees maintenance and other projects as well as handling the Yales' real estate properties.

"It's an awesome place to come to every day," said Cindy. "I love every minute of it! Chad's original concept was a place where families could come to shop, eat and play. The pieces of how we would accomplish that evolved as we worked with the architect. We're so proud of what we provide: a welcoming, family atmosphere with entertainment for all ages."

Business experts recommended the Yales build Sports World Stadium in a larger market and told them that Minot's size, population about 35,000, made the venture a financial risk, but Cindy explained, "It was very important to Chad that it be in Minot. He wanted to give back to the people who had given to us. We all knew Sports World Stadium's chances for real success were much better in a larger city, but we located it in Minot because this is the community that wrapped its arms around us."

Celebrating the facility's first anniversary last fall and now opening The Athlete's Foot in Sports World Stadium have been major milestones. The facility employs about 100 people, making it the city's 10th largest employer.

When the Yales were building the large complex, Cindy wrestled with personal pain caused by rumors critical of her family for building the facility to make more money and for their decision to sue the railroad.

"If financial reasons were the primary issue, we would have built Sports World Stadium in a larger market," Cindy asserted. "I don't think anyone would ever want to trade places with us. Chad, and all of us, have paid a huge price and we'd turn it all back, including Sports World Stadium, if we could turn back the hands of time. I'm not saying having the money isn't nice. But it's so immaterial to who we are."

The decision to sue the railroad was difficult, but made at the advice of attorneys who cautioned the Yales not to accept the railroad's position about providing for future expenses. No medical insurance will cover Chad; his condition increases the likelihood of future medical problems; and his physical limitations hamper his ability to provide for himself. The Yales' stress was intensified by media reports that published an inaccurate, exaggerated amount of money the Yales supposedly received from the railroad.

While Cindy wants to see the record set straight, she isn't willing to dwell on it. She chooses to hold on to the elements that steadied her through Chad's ordeal: a strong faith in God and a determined will to remain positive.

This year Cindy faced another hurdle: the empty nest syndrome. Chad and Scott both moved out of the family home. Chad shares a house with three friends. One of them is Bill, his best buddy from grade school and high school days.

"I could easily have cried as they left," Cindy said. "But it was a celebration for us. We didn't know when, or if, Chad would ever be able to live independently. It was good to realize he can, and we knew they both needed to move on with their lives."

Chad still has one more required surgery ahead of him. Other surgeries are possible if he opts to have reconstructive plastic surgery and a prosthesis for his arm.

Rocky and Cindy continue much as they have in the past. Their church is a strong force in their lives. Cindy is still a youth group leader, and is a member of the church council. Rocky is involved in a church building project as one of the general contractors. They enjoy attending local sports activities and rodeos, and traveling to watch national sports activities.

Cindy is excited about the opportunities presented by any profits generated from He is Alive! All profits go to Support Thru Sports, a foundation with Chad as chairman. Like the Minneapolis program that linked Chad with Greg Olson and other sports figures, Support Thru Sports will provide burn patients with sports mementos and interaction with athletes.

Cindy dreams of seeing Support Thru Sports benefit burn patients not only in the Midwest, but eventually throughout the United States. She envisions other Sports World Stadiums being built, and admits her family has been approached about making a movie to tell their story. But for now, she is content to enjoy the present and each day that it brings.

Each year as the February 27 anniversary date of Chad's accident approaches, Cindy simultaneously celebrates and struggles with the overwhelming emotions that take her back to a time and place in her life when simply existing was a day-to-day journey. Then, with the strong will that established her as the family rock in time of crisis, she forces herself to move on.

DATE DUE

FEB 1 5 '00			
APR 2 6 '00			
MAR			